Verbal Deficit

A CRITIQUE

J.C.B. GORDON

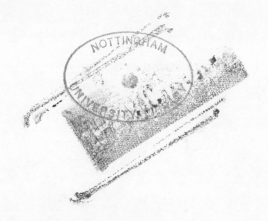

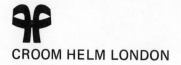

CROOM HELM LONDON

© 1981 J.C.B. Gordon
Croom Helm Ltd, 2-10 St John's Road, London SW11

British Library Cataloguing in Publication Data

Gordon, J.C.B.
   Verbal deficit.
   1. Psycholinguistics
   2. Sociolinguistics
   I. Title
   401'.9   P37

   ISBN 0-85664-990-2

To Leonore Betty Dorothea Gordon

Printed and Bound in the United States of America

CONTENTS

LESS COMMON ABBREVIATIONS

HMC   Headmasters' Conference

HMI   Her (or His) Majesty's Inspector [of Schools]

LCC   London County Council

LEA   Local Education Authority

ILEA   Inner London Education Authority

PGCE   Postgraduate Certificate in Education

NOTES ON THE USE OF THE 'HARVARD SYSTEM'

Readers may find it helpful to note the following conventions used in this book:

1.   Where reference is made to works written by different authors with identical surnames, the author cited most frequently is normally referred to by surname alone (together with date and, where necessary, letter) and the other author(s) are distinguished by initials immediately after the surname. In cases where two or more authors with identical surnames are cited equally frequently the author whose initial(s) place him or her first in alphabetical order is referred to by surname alone, and initials are given immediately after the surname for the others. Thus G. Collins is referred to simply as *Collins*, and R.N. Collins as *Collins, R.N.* In case of doubt, readers should consult the Bibliography.

2.   Edited works consisting of collections of articles by various authors are referred to by the names of the editor(s), followed by *ed.* or *eds.* in parentheses together with the year, for example: *Chanan and Delamont* (eds., 1975).

3.   In cases where authors published both as editors and individuals in the same year, the edited work is distinguished from the other by means of the convention described in para. 2. Thus Caroll (ed., 1956) and Carroll (1956) refer to separate bibliographical items, despite the fact that the latter is, in fact, the Introduction in the former.

INTRODUCTION

In view of the fact that there already exist a number of other writings which criticise verbal deficit theories, it may be helpful to begin by commenting on the nature and purpose of this present critique. It does not attempt to offer a comprehensive survey of all research on the subject of language, social class and education. Within the context of a wide-ranging and thorough study of sociolinguistics, Dittmar (1976) provides an excellent review of all the important research in this area published by about 1972, and Edwards (1979) has extended the coverage up to about 1979. Rather, my aim has been to break fresh ground and in particular to examine verbal deficit theories within a much broader context than has been attempted in earlier critiques.

One of the most noteworthy features of verbal deficit theories is their unstated assumptions. These are often not obvious and require thorough elucidation. I first endeavoured to set about this task in four articles, published between 1976 and 1978 (Gordon 1976a, 1976b, 1977 and 1978a) and in this book I have drawn on material from them, especially in Chapters 2 and 3. Elucidation is particularly important as it is largely on the basis of their implicit assumptions that verbal deficit theories stand or fall in scientific terms.

Although verbal deficit theories are often regarded as a branch of sociolinguistics they are in fact attempts to account, largely on the basis of linguistic or supposedly linguistic criteria, for the uneven distribution of educational attainment in society. In other words, despite their linguistic emphasis they ultimately belong to the sociology of education; in this critique they are examined in this context, as well as from a linguistic point of view.

The historical perspective adopted in Chapters 1 and 5 may surprise some readers. Such a perspective affords many advantages. It directs attention to the historical circumstances, to the political, social and economic climate in which theories are formulated, developed and accepted or rejected; this focus is essential in order to understand the function of a theory and explore the reasons for its dissemination and reception. In turn, an understanding of the function of a theory often provides valuable clues to any unstated premises which it may incorporate. Outside linguistics and sociology, the most popular rival to verbal deficit theories is not the linguistic variability hypothesis but still the psychometric intelligence theory. Partly for this reason, and partly because verbal deficit theories retain some of the assumptions of the psychometric intelligence theory, special attention is given in Chapter 1 to the circumstances in which the latter attained and subsequently lost a position of hegemony in educational theory in Britain.

I have made use of two interlocking modes of critique. The first, which is historical and sociological, is largely concerned with the functions of the main theories under discussion. This mode predominates in Chapters 1 and 5 and constitutes the general framework of the book. The second mode of critique is concerned with what verbal deficit theories claim, implicitly and explicitly, and with the scientific status and validity of these claims. The main sociolinguistic alternative to the verbal deficit theory — the linguistic variability hypothesis (or 'difference theory') — is also discussed from a similar point of view, though much more briefly. This second mode is used in the core of the book (Chapters 2–4). However, merely to demonstrate that a theory is unsound is not always entirely satisfactory, except in a purely philosophical sense. In order to illustrate the kind of phenomena that may lend credibility to verbal deficit theories I conducted a small-scale empirical study which is reported and discussed in Appendix 2.

At various points the ambiguity of the term *theory* has posed problems. At the one extreme, the term denotes a testable proposition or group of related propositions which have been thoroughly tested, especially at their apparently most problematical points, and have successfully withstood this process of testing. At the other extreme the term is more commonly used to refer to almost any set of ideas, whether speculative, ideological or scientific. I have not taken it upon myself to alter the now well-established designations of the various bodies of ideas under consideration. I hope that wherever the term *theory* is used its meaning will be clear from the context. A brief explanation is, however, required in connection with the expressions *(the) verbal deficit theory* and *verbal deficit theories*. I have used the former where it is necessary or appropriate to stress what the various concepts of verbal deficit have in common and the latter where recognition of the differences between various versions of the theory is necessary.

It is my hope that this book will be of equal interest to sociolinguists and educationalists, and I have tried to clarify the implications of verbal deficit theories (and various rival theories) for educational policy.

I would like to thank my wife, Janet Gordon, for her encouragement (and tolerance!) while I was writing this book. With her wide-ranging interests in the social sciences, she also provided many very valuable comments and suggestions. I am also grateful to those students, past and present, at the University of East Anglia who made many valuable comments and observations on various topics discussed in this critique. In particular, I would like to thank Ms Kathy Mulleague for her observations on the status of verbal deficit theories as a branch of the sociology of education and for highlighting their essentially non-linguistic character.

In writing this book I was also very fortunate in receiving advice, comments and suggestions given from several different stand-points. I wish to thank those who very kindly commented on the draft versions of various chapters — Professor Roger Fowler, Dr Leonard Jackson, Dr Stephen Wilson and Mrs Carole Woodruff. I should like to place on record my particular gratitude to two people who very kindly commented on nearly all the chapters in draft form, and who encouraged me throughout the writing of this book — Dr Gunta Haenicke and Professor Brian Simon. Responsibility for the final product, for the opinions which I express in it and for any errors rests, of course, entirely with me.

I wish to thank members of staff, and pupils, at the two schools where I made the tape-recordings used in Appendix 2. In the interests of maintaining the anonymity of the institutions and individuals concerned, they cannot be named. However, I should like to place on record my thanks and appreciation.

Among librarians, special thanks are due, to Miss Judith Kinsey, Mrs Ann Wood and her staff at the University of East Anglia, and to Mr Roy Kirk and his staff at the University of Leicester School of Education.

Thanks are also due to the University of East Anglia for granting me a term's study leave (Autumn Term 1979) while I was working on this book.

To Mrs June Harvey, Secretary at the Language Centre in the University of East Anglia, I am immensely grateful for typing several successive drafts of the manuscript, for dealing with much of the correspondence relating to this book and for producing an impeccable final typescript.

Finally a word about my mother, to whom this book is dedicated. Her views on a wide range of educational matters, expressed vigorously throughout my school career, and her willingness to discuss these views with me as a boy, did much to stimulate an early and lasting interest in education.

J.C.B. Gordon
University of East Anglia,
Norwich

Since verbal deficit theories are ultimately nothing more than attempts to account for differential educational attainment, it is essential to begin with a discussion of this more general area.

At various times in the history of mass education different explanations have been offered for the phenomenon called *differential educational attainment* — the fact that children who pass through an education system reach very different levels of attainment, as measured by the criteria in general use at the time. These differences are apparent not only in the qualifications obtained (and not obtained) by pupils on leaving the education system, but also in comparisons of children at any age-point within the system. To some extent such differences are also reflected in, and a result of, the age at which pupils leave the education system itself. The criteria currently used to measure or assess attainment are not confined to examinations and qualifications enjoying a measure of recognition among the general public (for example, the 11+, CSE, GCE 'O' and 'A' level examinations, diplomas and degrees) but also include tests devised specifically for the purpose of comparing large numbers of pupils in various skills and attainments at various ages (for example, the Watts-Vernon reading tests, NS6, Raven's Progressive Matrices). Most of these latter tests are largely unknown to the general public, and it is unusual for pupils or their parents to be informed of individual results on such tests. There also exist a number of aptitude tests whose stated aim is purely to establish pupils' suitability for certain kinds of courses. If such tests really measured pure aptitude, there might be a case for treating them as fundamentally different in kind from the tests discussed so far; but since they also measure attainment, if only indirectly in the form of (attained) ability to cope with formal tests, they should also be included in this list. Some such tests actually claim to test attainment in one skill on the grounds that it constitutes aptitude for another skill,[1] and in any case it is unclear exactly what aptitude tests really measure.

There are four kinds of answer which can be given to the general question: *Why do pupils passing through roughly the same (or apparently roughly the same) education system attain differently?* (Phenomenon I). The four types of answer are as follows, though they are not mutually exclusive and various combinations are often found:

1. With the exception of a small number of genuinely pathological cases, children enter school roughly equal in terms of educability. Differences in attainment, at least up to the end of the elementary stage of schooling, can largely be accounted for by (i) unevenness in the quality of teaching and (ii) differences, stemming from parental and peer-group influences, among the children themselves in their motivation to learn, their willingness to work and to accept the discipline of the school. In principle such differences are amenable to change within the education system itself. In this context, *elementary schooling* is defined not by any arbitrary age-limits nor as the teaching of basic skills, but as the whole period during which children share a broadly common curriculum.[2]

2. The material circumstances of the various parts of the education system itself and of the pupils vary enormously: (i) Some schools are good, others, bad, and others intermediate. Some are well-equipped, well accommodated, have effective teachers with high qualifications and a low rate of staff turnover, while at the other extreme the very opposite is the case. (ii) Some children suffer from material disabilities which tend to impair their efficiency in learning. They may be undernourished, underslept, inadequately clothed and poorly housed. Other children may suffer none of these disabilities and may be able to operate at optimum efficiency for most of the time they spend at school and may also have excellent facilities for learning out of school and for doing homework (for example, own books, own study, extensive foreign travel).

3. The children are significantly different in terms of educability when they first enter school. This difference is the result of (i) heredity, (ii) environment or (iii) a combination of both.

4. The various institutions within the education system (including the whole concomitant apparatus of examinations, tests, continuous assessment and qualifications) actually create academic success and failure, in 'good' establishments as well as 'bad'. Schools take in pupils who, with a handful of exceptions, are normal, healthy and educable and then systematically and inexorably turn them into successes and failures. According to this view success and failure are often seen as relatively meaningless labels, and it is often claimed that even those

who are nominally successful understand very little about the subjects in which they formally qualified.

These are, of course, only very general answers, and questions about individual pupils' performance in specific areas of examinations would have to be answered in rather different terms. As already noted, these explanations are not mutually exclusive.[3] In particular the first two explanations can be combined without doing any great violence to either. For example, Runciman (1887, pp. 45–6) implies a combination of the first two types of explanation in his description of the achievements and thoughts of the fictitious (?) model teacher, Palliser:

> The young master fought on stubbornly in his wretched shed; his efforts often failed, and in his first two years he had many a heartache. But his work was solid and useful, and his school finally became a favourite show-place, much frequented by gentlemen who wished to see 'how we deal with this kind of material'. Palliser knew that the material could be moulded to almost any form, and he was quite ready to match those of his lads who happened to be well fed against any boys from more favoured neighbourhoods. The starvation problem beat him, and it is likely to puzzle the nation for some years to come.[4]

However, the broad thrust of the four types of explanation is in each case distinct, despite the fact that the first two explanations are to some extent complementary. The first stresses the efficiency of the school, the second stresses the socially conditioned efficiency of the child in learning, the third is fundamentally deterministic, and the fourth treats success and failure as artefacts created by the education system itself. Since these are only broad thrusts, or categories of explanation, a range of interpretations is possible, especially in the case of the third and fourth explanations. The third explanation includes not only the intelligence theory, but also theories of linguistic determinism and those psychological theories which attach an overriding significance to the child's very early (and necessarily preschool) development. The fourth type of explanation comprises the relatively moderate view that schools create success and failure in order to ration access to various further steps on the educational ladder as well as the much more drastic suggestion that all educational establishments are intrinsically authoritarian and, as such, deeply corrupting; in this case the artificial creation of success and failure is seen as a prerequisite for maintaining and perpetuating the authoritarian hierarchy itself. However, of the four types of explanation, only the third invokes the concept of differential educability. In this crucial respect explanations of this kind are fundamentally different from all others, however much allowance they may make for environmental factors.

The matter does not end however with differential educational attainment as such (Phenomenon I). It is well known that *there is – and apparently has been for a long time – a close correlation between educational attainment and social status* (Phenomenon II). Broadly, the higher the parental rating on the Registrar-General's scale, the more likely a child is to succeed in all tests of attainment at all levels within the school system; and children with parents in unskilled manual occupations and those from certain ethnic minority groups tend to leave the education system as soon as is legally permitted (or earlier) and do so with few, if any, formal qualifications. As a group they perform least well on all tests of attainment currently in use. Also, these children are the most likely to be classified as failures, 'non-academic' or educationally subnormal (ESN) at a relatively early stage in their school-lives.

In principle, it is perfectly possible to advance hypotheses to account for Phenomenon I without any reference to social class whatsoever: indeed, this is exactly what has just been done. On the other hand, it is utterly impossible to venture any hypothesis on Phenomenon II without having some hypothesis to explain Phenomenon I, even if only on an implicit level.

In the course of the present century educationalists, sociologists, politicians and the general public have become increasingly conscious of Phenomenon II – the relationship between educational success and social class – and in the last twenty-five years or so it has become a matter of widespread preoccupation. Since all major political parties throughout the industrialised countries (and in some cases elsewhere, too) publicly proclaim their commitment to equality of opportunity via the education system, it is not surprising that the matter has become an overtly political question in most Western nations. Questions immediately arise as to whether an education system offers something approximating to real equality of opportunity or whether it is loaded in such a way as to preserve the privileges of the privileged and per-petuate the disabilities of those at the lower end of the social scale. Thus any hypothesis on Phenomenon I has political implications, because it is potentially a partial explanation for Phenomenon II.

Irrespective of whether or not an individual sees his explanation for
Phenomenon I as 'political', nothing can alter the fact that it will have
political implications.

Verbal deficit theories constitute a relatively recent attempt to
explain differential educational attainment. Some people still refer to
intelligence as if it were a self-evident, unassailable and virtually
sufficient explanation. They would be surprised to discover that, at
least in this country, it came into general fashion only in the early
1920s, and seem to forget that it has been under persistent and
mounting criticism since about 1950. The concept of intelligence as an
innate, fixed and measurable entity originated with the Social
Darwinists, in particular Galton (1865 and 1869), but had virtually no
impact on educational theory or practice till the mid-1880s at the
earliest; even then its real impact remained slight and fragmentary
till about 1918. For most of the nineteenth century differential
attainment was explained almost exclusively in terms of the quality of
teaching and also to some extent in terms of the moral qualities — real
or alleged — of the pupils and by implication also of their parents.
Although it is convenient in a British context to refer to such
explanations as *Victorian* the term is, strictly speaking, misleading
since the underlying ideas stemmed from the Enlightenment[5] and in
various forms were widely current in Protestant Europe, southern
Germany, France and, to some extent, Austria from the late
eighteenth century onwards. In *The Wealth of Nations*, for example,
Adam Smith had commented:

> The difference of natural talents in different men is, in reality,
> much less than we are aware of; and the very different genius which
> appears to distinguish men of different professions, when grown
> up to maturity, is not upon many occasions so much the cause
> as the effect of the division of labour. The difference between the
> most dissimilar characters, between a philosopher and a common
> street-porter, for example, seems to arise not so much from nature
> as from habit, custom, and education.[6]

To claim that the Victorians were *unaware* of differences in ability
which they often interpreted as natural or innate would be absurd.
Even Stow (1836) who stresses the need for systematic and effective
teaching in addition to mere exposition, the need for appropriately
designed, purpose-built schools and the importance of providing
suitable apparatus, refers to 'children of large and small capacities'[7]

and notes that within his proposed combined national system of
education for both the working and middle classes some children may
display different qualities early in life which will ultimately lead them
to different callings in society. However, there are only four, brief
references in the whole book to anything that can be interpreted as
differences in innate ability.[8] Dunn (1837, p. 3), quoting from
another writer, refers to pupils of 'every variety, both as to knowledge
and capacity', but it is the only such reference. Although most
modern readers will probably find Dunn's authoritarianism distasteful,
his book, like Stow's, is remarkable for its optimism regarding the
potential of education. For example, Dunn (1837, p. 12) observes,
'Children are, to a much greater extent than is generally supposed,
reasonable and intelligent beings . . . ' Neither David Stow nor Henry
Dunn were in any sense mere theorists; both were very active in their
respective educational societies (the Glasgow Educational Society
and the British and Foreign School Society) and had close contact
with actual schools.

It is important to distinguish intelligence as an everyday concept,
often applied to isolated actions and solutions to specific problems
or in a loose and general sense to persons, from the much narrower
and rigid psychometric concept of intelligence that arose from
Social Darwinism.[9] That the Victorians, along with other generations,
possessed the former, essentially functional concept of intelligence is
beyond doubt: indeed, in some form or other, this everyday concept is
a prerequisite for judging the actions of others. Moreover, the
Victorians were, of course, aware of idiocy and subnormality.[10] At the
other extreme much of their historiography, as well as their increasing
reliance on competitive examinations for the awarding of scholarships,
for appointments to some fellowships at Oxford and Cambridge and
to the Civil Service, together with the gradual mystification of the
First Class Honours degree, point to a widespread and growing concept
of brilliance, and even of genius in something approaching the modern
sense of the word. (Until relatively late in the nineteenth century the
word *genius* was generally used in its modern sense only in literary and
aesthetic criticism. It was more commonly used in the sense of
natural ability or predisposition − whether exceptional, outstanding,
or not.[11] Similarly, for much of the nineteenth century the word
intelligent was widely used in the sense of *rational, well-informed,
educated* or *discerning*, and *intelligence* in the sense of *reason*.)

Obviously, in the nineteenth century people did have a general
concept of (innate) intelligence, but apart from its everyday application,

the concept seems to have been largely confined to the extremes of subnormality and brilliance; no attempt was made to relate the concept in
any systematic way to the education system. The evidence for much
of this is fragmentary, as is often the case with the history of ideas,
especially as for most of the Victorian era mere attendance was as
much of a preoccupation as attainment. The evidence includes the
general absence, almost up to the very end of the century, of any discussion of intelligence in HMI's reports, the minutes of the Privy
Council Committee on Education, teacher-training manuals and other
writings on education.[12] This absence of references to intelligence in
teacher-training manuals tended to persist right up to the end of the
century. For example, although Salmon (1898, pp. 13–14) acknowledges that all children are not alike, there is no mention anywhere in
the book of intelligence (in its modern sense) or heredity. Like Stow
(1836), Salmon (1898) is concerned first and foremost with the
quality of teaching and the fundamental equality of educability of
all children.

But perhaps the most interesting piece of evidence is the Revised
Code of 1862 and its inauguration of the system of payment by
results which did not disappear completely till 1897. If the notion
that educability depended on intelligence had enjoyed any widespread
degree of support in the 1860s and the following two decades the
Revised Code would have appeared patently absurd, even as a drastic
economy measure; and one would have expected its critics (especially
the teaching profession itself) to have argued that payment by results
arbitrarily penalised those teachers who, irrespective of their
individual merits, had the misfortune to have a large number of
'unintelligent' children in their classes. In such a climate of opinion,
the adage that 'even the gods fight in vain against stupidity' would
have constituted a very powerful argument against the system.
However, in contemporary opposition to the Revised Code this line
of reasoning is conspicuous by its absence.[13] On the contrary, the
system of payment by results presupposed a wide measure of *equality*
of educability and placed the onus for ensuring attainment quite unambiguously on teachers. Some may argue that Lowe, who as Vice-
President of the Privy Council Committee on Education piloted the
Revised Code through Parliament, was less than fully honest about
its aims when he presented it as little more than an attempt to secure
economies or promote efficiency.[14] For example, Hurt (1972,
p. 202) comments:

In the final analysis, the promulgation and enforcement of the
Revised Code constituted a significant victory for the state in its
struggle with the Churches for control over education. No longer
was the state going to subsidize schools whose primary function
was to rear the young in the principles of the Christian faith.

But whatever subsidiary or covert motives may have played a part in
the formulation of the code, and however devious Lowe's behaviour
in 1861 and 1862 may have been, no-one has yet suggested that the
Education Department secretly subscribed to an intelligence theory
but deliberately suppressed it in public. In another important respect,
too, the Revised Code presupposed (perhaps fortuitously) the concept
of equality of educability. The actual mechanism by which results
were assessed for the purposes of payment involved the establishment
of six (later seven) 'standards' (I–VI/VII) in which pupils were
examined annually. Since no pupil could be presented more than once
in any given standard this led, as Simon (1967, p. 203) observes, to a
situation where 'Inevitably, wherever it was possible, classes were
organized according to the standards with the aim of promoting all
children annually, so that classes became known as Standard 1,
Standard 2, and so forth.' Implicit in this arrangement was the
assumption that children should progress smoothly through the six
standards in the space of six years and that, given reasonably
favourable circumstances, the vast majority were capable of doing
so.[15]

There is one piece of counter-evidence which must now be considered in some detail, namely Isaac Taylor's *Home Education*. (The
book was published anonymously, the first edition appearing in 1838,
the fifth in 1851, the seventh and last in 1867. The preface is dated
1837. All references below are to the fourth edition, published in
1842.) In at least two respects the book is polemical: the author seeks
to argue a general case for the potential advantages of home versus
school education and is particularly concerned to make a case for
keeping girls out of school. Taylor (1842) is also problematical for
other reasons. One of his principal aims is to devise an enlightened
scheme of education for his own children,[16] and his position is to
some extent defensive. The book was first written at a time when the
existing public schools (in 1837 the nine Clarendon Schools) and the
endowed grammar schools were largely failing to cater for the needs
of the new middle class. From the early 1840s onwards this problem
was gradually overcome by the establishment of new proprietary

boarding schools, beginning with Cheltenham (1841), Marlborough
(1843) and Rossall (1844), and by the growth of a wide range of
proprietary day-schools. The initial popularity of the book, followed
by the relatively long gap between the publication of the fourth
and fifth editions, may indicate that soon after 1842 the author's
preoccupations, at least as far as boys were concerned, were rapidly
losing their immediate relevance. It is also possible to interpret the
author's defensiveness as an attempt to isolate the bourgeois household from the public world.[17] Despite these difficulties Taylor (1842)
is an educational work of substance, in some respects highly percep-
tive, and must be taken seriously.

Unlike the teacher-training manuals examined, Taylor (1842)
contains a number of references to such things as differences in
'capacities' (p. 8), 'the substantial benefits of classification which
consist in the treatment of each according to his capacities' (p. 89),
'general ability' (p. 197) and 'minds of a thoroughly ordinary
stamp' (p. 201). Indeed, Taylor (1842, p. 9) argues that one of the
main advantages of home education is precisely that it can and
ought to cater for such differences, to the advantage of the pupils:
'in diversifying the methods of teaching, in accordance with the
capacities of those who are to be taught, much may be effected at
home which could not be admitted at school . . . '

Taylor does not see differences in ability as an explanation for
differential educational attainment. Between 1838 and 1842, and
subsequently, there were no agreed criteria of academic attainment
other than basic literacy at the one extreme and university degrees
at the other. The only readily available criteria of success and failure
at the time were economic and perhaps the attainment of public
office. In connection with these, Taylor (1842, pp. 208–9) notes, or
claims, a widespread discrepancy between success at school (as
judged informally by teachers and fellow-pupils) and subsequent
economic and public success. Even if one makes allowances for anti-
school polemics on the part of the author, his remarks on this are
probably a reasonably accurate reflection of the absence of any distinct nexus at that time between academic education and employment,
except in the case of a handful of professions.

Although Taylor does not, of course, propose a psychometric
intelligence theory he goes beyond the 'everyday' concept of
intelligence discussed above and well beyond the passing comments
made on the subject of differences in innate ability by Stow (1836),
Dunn (1837), Collins, R.N. (1843) and other educational writings of

the period. This becomes especially clear if one notes the fact that he expresses many ideas that are concomitant with intelligence theories. He subscribes to much which by about 1940 had become educational orthodoxy. Taylor (1842, pp. 201–11) draws a sharp distinction between 'intellectual' and 'non-intellectual' minds, the former being, broadly speaking, suited to a classical education, the latter not; and he expresses the view that the curriculum should be child-centred at least in the minimum sense that it should to a large extent be determined by the child's aptitudes, tastes and ability (as perceived by the educator). One passage in Taylor (1842, p. 191) is particularly remarkable:

> as early as the eleventh year, or at some time during the middle period of the educational course, enough may ordinarily be known of children's natural endowments to enable a parent to assign them, severally, to one or the other of the two classes — the intellectual, who are to receive an elaborate and extended culture; or the un-intellectual, who are to be fitted for business or business-like engagements, and whose education, of whatever sort, may well be brought to a close at an early age.

With a few minor modifications (above all, the substitution of *one* for *a parent* and some reference to 'expert witnesses') this passage might as well have been lifted from any major government report on school education from Hadow (1931) to Norwood (1943)! From a historical point of view, the key point is that Isaac Taylor offered the basis for an intelligence theory and its concomitant assumptions, *but the offer was not taken up*. The fact that Victorian educational thinking did not develop along these lines merely highlights the fact that in general the Victorians had, quite literally, no use for an intelligence theory in education. What happened in practice was that upper-class and upper-middle-class boys, whether 'intellectual' or not, tended to receive an academic education at the 'public schools' (including the new proprietary boarding schools and former grammar schools turned into public schools) or at home, working-class children received rudimentary education in elementary schools, while a variety of other institutions catered for the strata in between.

Taylor (1842, p. 6) states his basic concept of education is in-compatible with equitable school education:

> It is true that a sedulous and conscientious teacher, or an ambitious

one, from other motives, may take pains to adapt his usual methods
of training to the taste and capacity of certain individuals, under
his care, lending aid to the feeble, and bestowing especial care
upon the intelligent; but it might well be questioned, in such cases,
whether the eighteen out of twenty are not losers to the whole
amount of the peculiar regard that is given to the one or two . . .
School training, to be equitable, must be a training of minds in the
mass.

To dismiss this as a form of special pleading would be facile, for in
fact this view, with only slight modifications, seems to have dominated
school teaching at virtually all levels until the closing years of the
nineteenth century and, in the elementary sector, even beyond 1900.
Moreover the fundamental question raised by Taylor in this passage
has been raised again in the present century in respect of the education
system as a whole.

Galton (1869) advanced an uncompromisingly hereditarian
intelligence theory within the framework of a general theory of Social
Darwinism. He saw intelligence as an innate, immutable and, in
principle, measurable attribute determining the entire range of
the individual's potential for intellectual and cognitive development,
and he was the first person to attempt to define various levels of
intelligence statistically. For these reasons he is rightly regarded as
the founder of the psychometric theory of intelligence. But despite
the subsequent publication of Galton (1883) which sought to develop
the theory further, Galton and his Social Darwinist philosophy had
virtually no impact on educational theory or practice until the very
end of the century. (An interesting exception is Kingsley (1874,
pp. 1–25) who ruminates along Social Darwinist lines about the
'degeneration of the race'. However, the only conclusion he draws is
that children should be taught basic biology and personal hygiene,
and he does not discuss Galton's intelligence theory at all.)   Until the
mid-1890s, and to a large extent beyond, the kind of ideas proposed
by Galton remained largely confined to a very small number of
people concerned with biology and medicine and the then proto-
sciences of psychology and physical anthropology. Educationalists
remained almost entirely outside this circle.

Just as the early Victorian educationalists did not take up Taylor's
intelligence theory, mid- and late Victorian educationalists largely
ignored Galton's theory. However, towards the end of the nineteenth
century notions of differential educability gradually forced their way

into educational theory and, to a lesser extent, practice. The impetus
came from two quite separate sources, both severely practical, and
initially had nothing to do with Galton's theory. Practice came first,
and theory was subsequently utilised in order to justify it. The trend
towards compulsory schooling in the last three decades of the century,
backed up by a greater degree of enforcement, brought into the
elementary schools an increasing number of physically and mentally
handicapped or retarded children of a kind who had previously not, it
seems, caused serious problems.[18] Presumably they had either
escaped compulsion, dropped out, or to some extent been helped over
their difficulties by conscientious and sympathetic teachers. By the
late 1880s these children came to be seen as a distinct problem within
the school system, but effective action to make special provision for
such children was very slow, despite the passing of the Elementary
Education (Blind and Deaf Children) Act in 1893 and the Elementary
Education (Defective and Epileptic Children) Act of 1899. (The
latter was purely permissive and was not replaced by a more effective
Act until 1914.)

The second impetus came from a very different source and is much
more complex. During the last two decades of the nineteenth century
some education authorities made increasing provision for post-
elementary education (usually in 'higher grade' or technical schools).
This development had begun before 1880 in Leeds, Sheffield,
Manchester and Birmingham, but after 1889—90 various kinds of
cheap or free post-elementary education were made increasingly
available, above all in major industrial cities, some other county
boroughs and in London. Despite temporary local bottle-necks, it
was generally possible to avoid serious discrepancies between the
supply of such facilities and effective demand for them, because the
local authorities concerned (School Boards and County Borough
Councils, both often independently active in this field in one and the
same town) were in a position to raise or gain access to the
necessary money themselves. In 1900, however, the Court of Queen's
Bench ruled that the London School Board could not use any part
of the School Board rate to finance such education, and in 1901
this ruling was upheld in an even more drastic form by the Court of
Appeal, despite ambiguities in the 1870 Act.[19]

A detailed discussion of the 1902 Education Act and the various
events leading up to it is neither necessary, nor appropriate,
especially as the subject is treated in considerable detail and from
different points of view in a number of readily accessible histories

of the English education system, notably Curtis and Boultwood (1964, pp. 94–103 and 162–74), Simon (1965, pp. 176–246) and Lowndes (1969, pp. 39–74). It is sufficient to note that after 1902 the manner and extent to which any local education authority could finance any form of post-elementary education was in many respects much more closely regulated than had been the case between 1870 and 1900. This, together with a rapidly growing demand for various forms of secondary education, produced a growing mis-match between supply and demand which became acute in and after 1918. In these circumstances the question of the means of selection for secondary education was inevitably thrust into the fore.

Between 1902 and 1945 the relationship between supply and demand for secondary (that is, grammar school and various kinds of technical) education in the state sector was regulated in three ways: by parental ability to pay fees, by competitive examination and by increasing the supply, but the last of these regulators was subject to legal and financial constraints. When the relevant sections of the 1944 Education Act came into operation in April 1945, fees were abolished in the state sector and local education authorities were placed under a legal obligation to provide secondary education for all. Various plans for universal multilateral comprehensive secondary schooling were projected in some areas and actually realised in the Isle of Man by 1947 and Anglesey by 1952, but elsewhere were thwarted until the 1960s. Most local education authorities merely added a further year to their existing (senior) elementary schools, which they then labelled *secondary modern schools*, and developed or established a few intermediate and/or experimental kinds of institutions, including a few comprehensive schools operating in open competition with grammar schools. (The first such comprehensive school was established at Windermere in 1945.) Some authorities also increased the number of grammar school places. The great divide between elementary and secondary education continued in the form of the division between secondary modern and grammar schools, even in those areas where schools of an intermediate status were provided. Unless a local authority reorganised its entire post-primary school system on comprehensive lines, the only means of regulating supply and demand was either to increase grammar school provision to the point where it at least approximately met demand (as in some Welsh counties) or to rely primarily on competitive examination.

Thus, between 1902 and about 1960 the official view generally amounted to a blunt denial that the vast majority of schoolchildren were fit for anything other than a sub-standard, sub-academic education.[20] This doctrine called for a plausible ideological justification. The psychometric intelligence theory provided just that — and remarkably successfully too, until the mid-to-late 1950s. It is no coincidence that theories of differential educability, which had been available but largely ignored throughout the Victorian Era, gradually began to enter educational theory in the early years of the twentieth century.

The period between about 1875 and 1920 saw the gradual development in Britain and elsewhere of an attempt to establish the study of education as an academic discipline in its own right — even a science, and it was in this period that the first university Departments of Education were established in Britain. The rise of education as a university discipline owed much to the development of psychology in the last quarter of the nineteenth century; the majority of major academic works on education written in this period were primarily concerned with educational psychology and the psychology of child development, although there was often an admixture of philosophy, frequently of a highly speculative nature. On the whole, earlier theoretical works had tended to be more general and more philosophical in orientation. It can be argued that education acquired its new status largely by means of a 'sell-out' to psychology. Of course, teacher training manuals still continued to appear in large numbers and for a long time they remained almost entirely practical in character, largely unaffected by the new developments in educational theory. Among the last important manuals of this kind are Garlick (1896 and later editions) and Salmon (1898). In general there was a considerable time-lag between the formulation of theories and their dissemination among the mass of teachers in training. Ultimately, too, many major theorists also wrote books aimed at a wider readership and gradually these tended to supplant the earlier kind of manual.

Of the various schools of thought that emerged within educational theory in the period *c.* 1895—1920 two became particularly influential: the psychometric school and the child-centred school. There is sometimes a tendency to see these two schools as standing in opposition to one another, the former being regarded as orthodox or even conservative, the latter as progressive. This view is highly misleading. By 1930 at the latest the two had achieved a remarkable, symbiotic relationship. Both stressed differences rather than similarities between children and the fundamental notion that education should be fitted to the child's natural aptitudes was central to both schools of thought.

It is no coincidence that the major British proponents of child-centred education subscribed unquestioningly and enthusiastically to psychometry. This symbiosis is epitomised in the writings of Susan Isaacs, in particular Isaacs (1932a and 1932b).

The intelligence theory did not, however, arise within educational theory itself, nor did it occupy a position of pre-eminence among educationalists in the period between about 1895 and 1920, though the appointment in 1913 of Cyril Burt, a convinced psychometrist, to the newly created post of educational psychologist at the LCC was a portent of future developments. As far as educational theory was concerned, the whole period was one of transition and even confusion as the orthodoxies of the nineteenth century gradually disintegrated. For much of this period, too, the influence of both the psychometric and child-centred schools of thought was to some extent counterbalanced by Herbartians[21] like Adams, Dodd, Hayward and Welton. The Herbartians popularised the educational theories of the German philosopher, Johann Friedrich Herbart (1776–1841). Herbart was inclined to accept Locke's concept of the *tabula rasa* and, accordingly, laid great stress on the formative potential of education and the importance of systematic instruction. He also attached particular importance to moral education and the need to broaden the child's intellectual horizons. Not surprisingly, his followers in Britain in the late nineteenth and early twentieth centuries were generally not in sympathy with the intelligence theory, but on the whole they were not actively hostile either: some seem to have felt that psychometry was irrelevant to their educational theories and practices and only a handful saw the intelligence theory as a potential threat. The intelligence theory emanated from that particular brand of psychology which formed an integral part of Social Darwinism.

In 1901 Galton, together with Pearson, launched a systematic campaign to propagate Social Darwinist ideology. In view of the scale of the campaign (lavishly funded by Galton himself) and the fact that it attracted a measure of support among some intellectuals it is legitimate to speak of a 'Eugenics Movement' in Britain from 1901 up to about the beginning of the First World War, despite the fact that there were considerable differences of opinion among the eugenists. The ultimate aim of the movement was to improve the physical and mental quality of 'the race'. This term sometimes referred to the human species, but much more commonly, 'the British' or 'the English'. Summarised briefly, the chief aim was to accelerate the evolutionary process of natural selection by introducing a measure of planned or

artificial selection. The reason the eugenists offered for this was that
advances in medicine, the rise of industrial civilisation, and various
forms of social and fiscal legislation were preventing the process of
natural selection from operating properly: they claimed that among
the weak, those suffering from certain hereditary (or supposedly
hereditary) diseases, among the feeble-minded and a whole range of
people who for one reason or another they regarded as undesirable,
the birth-rate was being artificially prevented from falling; while on
the other hand such things as the domestic rating system, income
tax and death duties were allegedly preventing the strong and
intelligent from breeding to full capacity. The eugenists took it as
axiomatic that English society had been sufficiently fluid for long
enough to ensure that by and large the strong and intelligent had
risen to the top of society while the weak and stupid had sunk to the
bottom. On this basis they claimed that natural selection had already
assigned most people to their natural place in society.[22] While it is
important not to ascribe a greater measure of unity to the Eugenics
Movement than it actually possessed, the following passage by
Schuster (1913, pp. 225–6) illustrates the attitude of many eugenists
at that time towards education and equality of opportunity:

> In every walk of life there are opportunities for a man to rise, and
> in most the qualities which will enable him to take advantage of
> them depend to some extent on mental capacity.
> It may be that the opportunities sometimes favour moral
> attributes of an anti-social kind, but they never favour a weak
> intellect; the predatory millionaire is perhaps ethically of the
> same standing as the burglar, but intellectually he far surpasses him.
> It may be that in some cases sheer good fortune forces one man
> up, and sheer ill fortune brings another man down. It is also
> possible that some deficiency in hardness of character keeps
> success away from a man who would otherwise win it . . .
> To turn to arguments of a different nature, the London County
> Council sets up educational ladders in all parts of the Metropolis,
> but finds it difficult to get boys to go up them. The number of
> children in the schools maintained by the rates who are bright
> enough to make it worth while to give them the scholarships
> provided by the London ratepayer is hardly enough to fill them.
> No difficulty is experienced in filling those at the Public Schools
> or University with boys of a very respectable level of intelligence,
> whose fathers belong mostly to the professional classes. This is

a rough and vague method of comparison which, though not in itself very convincing, is put forward as deserving of thought.

Here was an ideology which — especially if presented in a duly expurgated form — was ideally suited to resist demands for the extension of genuinely secondary education to all.

Between 1861 and the mid-1880s Parliament, acting sometimes directly, sometimes through various statutory bodies, had relieved the endowed schools — whether of the 'public', grammar or hospital variety — almost completely of the remnants of their original function of providing free education for the poor.[23] The official reasons given for this massive misappropriation of public funds for the benefit of the upper and middle classes were that the endowed schools were inefficient in terms of the number of free places actually provided in relation to the level of endowment income, that many of the schools were corrupt, that they had quaint statutes which allowed for patronage and other abuses. But the chief justification offered was that working-class children quite simply did not *need* the kind of education provided by these schools. After the turn of the century, many eugenists like Schuster, Spearman and somewhat later Burt and Nunn, along with many politicians and senior civil servants, were to claim that most working-class children not only did not need the same kind of education as middle-class children but also that with only a handful of exceptions they were congenitally incapable of benefiting from it. This view tended to persist until the middle of the present century and well beyond. Analysing the findings of Burt (1943a), Nunn (1945, p. 134) wrote: 'We must infer, then, that 5 or 6 children out of every 1,000 in the "unskilled" class possess mental ability of at least scholarship standard.'

In the 1920s the psychometric intelligence theory achieved hegemony within a mere decade. It received a fulsome accolade of approval in the Hadow Report (1931), and later in an even more decisive form in the Spens Report (1938), which formed the main basis for the Education Act of 1944. Its rise to hegemony was easy, swift and almost total: psychometric theory became the new orthodoxy at all significant levels — at the Board of Education, among LEAs, in official reports and other government publications on education, in educational theory, in teacher training manuals and, if only because of the increasingly widespread use of group intelligence tests for secondary school selection, in schools. In short, within the space of a few years it achieved an iron grip on educational theory and practice which was not undermined in

any significant way until the early 1950s and is still not completely
broken. How did this sudden victory come about?

First, between 1918 and 1920 the discrepancy between the supply
of and demand for secondary school places reached hitherto un-
precedented proportions. Indeed, the situation was so acute that even
children whose parents were able and willing to pay fees had to be
turned away.[24] The state would either have to make a very substantial
increase in the number of secondary school places available, as
recommended in the *Report of the Departmental Committee on
Scholarships and Free Places* (1920), or find a plausible excuse for not
doing so. In the event the government pleaded the need for drastic
economy, refused to increase the number of places, and even went so
far as to enforce a temporary reduction.

Secondly, in 1916 Terman had succeeded in devising the first group
intelligence test that could plausibly be passed off as an objective test
of intelligence and that was easy to administer (the Stanford-Binet
test). The significance of this was enormous, since it facilitated the
process of expurgation referred to above. Earlier group intelligence
tests had been either unwieldy or transparently arbitrary and subjective.
Galton (1869) had based his case largely on a study of degrees of
kinship within the English judiciary and among British politicians.
Despite all attempts, especially by Pearson from the early 1890s onwards, to develop the statistical side of the theory, Galton and
Schuster (1906) still found themselves in the embarrassing position
of having to present their case in the form of a study of 'noteworthy
families'. Anything that smacked so obviously of class-bias and even
sycophancy, or anything as brutal and speculative as the passage from
Schuster (1913) quoted above, or even the early contributions of Burt,
Nunn and Spearman to the *Eugenics Review* and other periodicals
before the First World War, would probably have failed to win widespread acceptance in the 1920s. After 1916, however, it was possible
to present the theory without reference to anything of an overtly
Social Darwinist nature and the Social Darwinist ideology was buried
amid increasingly complex statistical operations, scarcely comprehensible to the layman. Moreover, one originally eugenist feature of
the theory was given a meritocratic, even pseudo-socialist twist. The
Eugenics Movement had claimed that among the working classes there
were a handful of children of well above-average intelligence and that
it was in the interests of 'the race' to provide them with secondary
education and recruit them to the middle class. After 1918 the
psychometrists were able to reformulate this aspect of the theory as
providing a potential path to equality of opportunity via the supposedly

culture-free group intelligence test. In the early 1920s several popular accounts of the theory were published, some containing actual tests. Important examples include Ballard (1920, 1922 and 1923), Burt (1921 and 1923) and Kennedy-Fraser (1923). In addition, a major official report, the *Report of the Consultative Committee on Psychological Tests of Educable Capacity* (1924), was broadly sympathetic.

Thirdly, the post-war boom of 1919–21 turned into a slump in 1921. While the rest of the industrialised nations enjoyed a period of relative prosperity for much of the 1920s, this was not the case in Britain, where the interwar slump lasted for the whole period from 1921 to 1940. (There were, of course, fluctuations and the depression was at its most severe in 1921–2 and 1930–4.) The economic policy of all the governments of this period was one of rigid monetarism. One direct result of this was that between 1921 and 1938 the annual intake of pupils into secondary schools in the state sector in England and Wales only rose from 95,561 (in 1921) to 98,820 (in 1938). Admittedly, the total number of places rose from 336,836 (1921) to 470,003 (1938) as more pupils stayed in secondary education longer, and the proportion of those holding free places also rose.[25] However, even this expansion of the state secondary sector was modest and fell far short of the 720,000 secondary school places recommended by the *Report of the Departmental Committee on Scholarships and Free Places* (1920). The indirect effects of the slump are more difficult to assess. Like all prolonged slumps, that from 1921 to 1940 tended to induce a widespread spirit of fatalism – precisely the kind of intellectual climate which was to prove highly receptive to psychometry with its deterministic and static view of human capabilities.

One of the most curious features of the hegemony of the intelligence theory is that there was a period of forty years during which not one British educationalist attacked it, though some expressed misgivings or tried to circumvent it. In Britain the only real challenge came from the biologist Hogben (1933 and 1938, pp. 331–3), and even that fell short of outright rejection. At the time of the Eugenics Movement, Hayward, a prominent Herbartian, had attacked the theory directly in a series of lectures delivered in 1907 which were published as a book in 1908. Hayward (1908, p. 4) wrote:

The old-fashioned metaphor of the *tabula rasa*, the old-fashioned philosophy of the impressionability of man, may be more true than

the new-fashioned metaphor of the plant, the new-fashioned
philosophy of the unchangeableness of character. Environment and
education may be well-nigh omnipotent . . . when compared with
heredity.

Hayward's use of the terms *old-fashioned* and *new-fashioned* is
significant, as it indicates the approximate time when the intelligence
theory was first perceived by any prominent educationalist in this
country as a threat to education. Of course, Hayward did not yet find
it necessary to write about the actual application of intelligence
testing in schools as this only began to take place after the First
World War.[26] Hayward (1908, p. 137) foreshadows modern criticisms
of the intelligence theory when he doubts whether intelligence actually
exists: 'Let the reader note that things have been attributed to heredity
that may have absolutely no existence at all.' Surprisingly, his
hostility to the theory weakened very quickly.[27] As for the other
leading Herbartians, Dodd hardly concerned herself with the question
of intelligence, while Adams's writings are characterised by prevarication
throughout his career as an educationalist.[28] His scepticism — and it is
little more than that — finds its clearest expression in Adams (1912,
pp. 302–4). Welton (1911, pp. 101–37) flirted with the theory but he
later expressed scepticism.[29]

   Between about 1920 and 1950 the intelligence theory exercised
such a grip on educational thinking that it was almost universally
accepted, even by the Left, and substantively undermined the campaign
for secondary education for all which gradually gained momentum in
the 1920s; until 1950 there was confusion even among members of the
Communist Party.[30] They were obviously unaware that the use of
intelligence tests in schools had been banned by decree in the Soviet
Union in 1936. Their ignorance of this was surprising in view of the
fact that a full English translation of the decree which condemned
psychometry in general had been published in Simon, E.D. *et al.*
(1937, pp. 130–5). Similarly, at that time no-one in Britain seems to
have taken note of the fact that the theory had been challenged in
the early 1920s by Walter Lippmann[31] in the USA or to have paid
any attention to Bagley (1925), published in the USA. One of the most
prominent campaigners for secondary education for all, Tawney
(1931, pp. 47 and 195–6) actually expressed admiration for Burt's
tests. In view of the fact that Tawney played a major part in the
formulation of the Labour Party's policy on education for much of
the interwar period, the effect of his uncritical acceptance of

psychometry should not be underrated.

At this point it may be useful to clarify a widespread misconception about the relationship between the theoretical implications of psychometry and the divided (tripartite or bipartite) system of secondary school provision. The psychometric intelligence theory does not, in itself, call for a division of secondary education along tripartite lines corresponding to modern, technical and grammar schools; still less does the theory justify the notion that there are three types of mind corresponding to the typical curricula of these types of school. This point was made forcibly by Burt (1943b) and Fleming (1947 and 1948, pp. 118–40). Since it is an axiom of psychometry that the distribution of intelligence among the population corresponds to a normal curve it could, for example, be argued that the psychometric intelligence theory points to the provision of élite schools for the 2 per cent with the highest IQs, special schools for the 2 per cent with the lowest IQs and a common comprehensive school for the remaining 96 per cent. Given the premises of the theory, it could reasonably be claimed that it is futile to differentiate in intelligence among pupils within the vast mass of the population. However, psychometrists have not argued for a policy so consistent with their axioms.

Of the government reports on education issued up to 1944 the only one to argue in terms of 'types of mind' was the Norwood Report (1943). Nevertheless the psychometrists had, at least indirectly, done much to foster such notions: first, by their persistent tendency to claim that a specified minimum IQ was a virtual prerequisite for ability to profit from a given type of curriculum (for example, an IQ of at least 115 for a conventional grammar school course); and secondly, by claiming that their intelligence tests could measure such prerequisites accurately and fairly. The Spens Report (1938), in rejecting the case for multilateral comprehensive schools (except on a very limited, experimental basis) and in recommending that secondary education should be organised almost exclusively on the tripartite system of modern, technical high and grammar schools, implicitly foreshadowed the Norwood ideology of types of mind. In a highly critical assessment of the operation of the 1944 Education Act after the war, Lady Simon of Wythenshawe (1948, p. 30), who had served on the Spens Committee, wrote:

The tripartite or unilateral [as opposed to multilateral or comprehensive] system rests on the assumption that there are roughly three types of children, academic, technical and the 'also rans'. These latter, it is said, need a general education, more practical in its approach and with a generous allowance of handwork. Both the Spens Committee and the Norwood Committee based their recommendations on this assumption.

Although the Spens Report (1938) paved the way for the 1944 Education Act, which required LEAs to provide secondary education for all, the Norwood Report (1943) exercised a very considerable influence on the actual interpretation placed on the Act by the Ministry of Education and by the great majority of LEAs. Why, in view of Burt's exposure of the theoretical absurdity of the Norwood 'types of mind' ideology, did so many psychometrists actively collaborate with the administration (especially of the selection procedures) of a school system which was largely an embodiment of that ideology? The three types of mind were a psychological fiction, but this fiction functioned as a guise for designating three social strata – (i) the professional, (ii) highly skilled manual and (iii) less skilled manual strata – which the Norwood Report (1943), in effect, sought to keep distinct and separate. Since the concept of a close and necessary correlation in British society between social status and intelligence has always been central to psychometry and indeed forms the very basis of the Galtonian paradigm, the problems that the Norwood ideology posed for psychometry were apparent rather than real, and in many respects trivial.

In 1944 the concept of secondary education for all had apparently carried the day, but only at the cost of accepting a reinterpretation of the concept of secondary education which had the effect of diluting it to the point where it was easy to continue to operate within the kind of framework established already in 1902. As noted above, the great divide within the state sector largely continued, often in an only slightly modified form, except in a very small number of LEAs, mainly in sparsely populated areas, where practical considerations were often of overriding importance.

In view of the psychometrists' hegemony and the apparent impossibility of attacking them directly, the only alternative was to have recourse to a different frame of reference. At least two educationalists attempted to do this. Ironically, the first such attempt was made by a prominent psychometrist. Thomson (1929) disagreed in many respects with his colleagues; he stressed the importance of 'the social inheritance'[32] and in view of uncertainties in the biological basis of the intelligence theory regarded it as equal in importance, for most practical purposes, to biological inheritance. He concluded that in view of this, and in view of the need to create social solidarity, there should be one common school for all normal children from 5 to 15. After considering the various objections, Thomson (1929, pp. 274—5) suggested a school system designed primarily to create social solidarity:

> the social solidarity of the whole nation is more important than any of the defects to which a comprehensive high school may be subject, and which may in any case be ameliorated if not abolished. To have memories of life together in common, to have worn the same school cap, have played in the same team, will mean much for men and women even although they may not at school have been of the same intellectual level, and may have enjoyed different courses. And in a comprehensive school, under one head, there are many more chances of transferring a child from one course to another, if he be found to possess talent of a kind not at first suspected; and thus the nightmare of being tested and judged once and for all at the tender age of 11, and made or marred for life, will be removed for good.

The underlying reasoning here goes considerably further than was common at that time among others who advocated 'multiple-bias' schools (in other words, what would now be called streamed or setted comprehensive schools). Thomson's concept of education attracted little support at the time. It was, however, taken up again by Clarke (1940 and 1941). In particular Clarke (1941) advocates, fairly explicitly, a complete re-orientation and reorganisation of education as national service. He states that the recommendations of both the Hadow Report (1926) and the Spens Report (1938) fail to ensure adequate educational provision and favours the creation of a National Youth Service embracing the entire adolescent population up to age 18, with schooling obviously occupying a central but by no means exclusive role:

> For we are now contemplating with serious practical intent the initiation for all adolescents alike of forms of educative control to operate at least up to the age of 18 and perhaps later. The strikingly new feature of this most recent phase of thinking is not the extension of control to a later age, but the contemplation

of agencies of control other than the school, whether full-time or part-time. When we begin to speak, in terms of national organization, of clubs, community centres, sports, expeditions, forms of social service and active participation in industry as modes of public education which the State is prepared to subsidize, it would be well if we realized a little more clearly what we are doing. For, in effect, it is something of momentous importance, being nothing less than the reawakening . . . of the ideal of an Educative Society.[33]

Thomson (1929) and Clarke (1941) do not challenge the intelligence theory directly. Instead, they insist that there are things in education that are ultimately more important than differences in either intelligence or attainment. But as they circumvent the intelligence theory they do not offer any alternative explanation for differential attainment. Before considering the first direct attacks on the theory, a few comments must be made on the hegemony of the intelligence theory. It was not, of course, the case that by 1930 all earlier ideas on the reasons for differential attainment had vanished completely. Although little remained of the Victorian concept of equality of educability, and although the stress on quality of teaching was diluted, the view that differential attainment was to some extent due to the moral attributes of the pupils did not disappear. At present no systematic research has been undertaken on school reports, but throughout this period there seems still to have been a strong tendency to moralise about academic performance. The hegemony of the intelligence theory operated above all at the levels of educational theory, official thinking and teacher training. In the schools themselves the theory led to rigid classification, but beyond that it is difficult to assess to what extent it influenced day-to-day teaching. Moreover, one teacher training manual, Ward and Roscoe (1928),[34] does not mention the intelligence theory at all, and in the brief section on 'the dunce' (pp. 32–4) displays much the same kind of optimism as many Victorian manuals. (Indeed many sections of the book have much in common with Blakiston (1879).)

One of the first notes of dissent came in 1947 when the Advisory Council on Education in Scotland reported on the means for implementing the Education (Scotland) Act of 1945 (the Scottish equivalent of the 1944 Act for England and Wales). In its Report[35] the Advisory Council notes that since at least 1872 provision for secondary education in Scotland had been much more generous than in England and Wales, largely because Scottish School Boards and municipal authorities had not been subject to the same stringent legal restrictions as their English and Welsh counterparts. The Report (1947, p. 1) suggests that partly as a result of this, 'Historically there had never been in Scotland such a complete separation of elementary and secondary education as in the Southern Kingdom . . . ' In rejecting the English tripartite system, the Report (1947, p. 31) states *inter alia*:

> The whole scheme rests on an assumption which teacher and psychologist alike must challenge – that children of twelve sort themselves out neatly into three categories to which these three types of school correspond. *It is difficult enough to assess general ability at that age*: how much harder to determine specific bents and aptitudes with the degree of accuracy that would justify this three-fold classification. (Italics – JCBG)

At the same time there was growing disappointment in England with the actual outcome of the 1944 Education Act. Finally, in the autumn of 1949 came the first outright rejections of the intelligence theory from any English educationalist since 1908 – Simon (1949a and 1949b) and Simon, J. (1949). These were followed by Morris (1951) and two years later Simon (1953) provided a detailed, thorough and intellectually devastating critique which exposed the theory underlying group intelligence testing as nothing more than a pseudo-science. No psychometrist has yet provided an adequate answer to this critique.

That these critiques of the intelligence theory, in particular Simon (1953), found a hearing and ultimately influenced educational policy owes much, of course, to their precision and thoroughness. However, this alone does not provide an adequate explanation for their success. At least two other, interrelated factors facilitated the dethroning of the psychometric intelligence theory at the time. First, and most importantly, the period from 1940 to 1973 (taken as a whole) saw a steady rise in economic output in Britain and elsewhere, and this prolonged boom required an increase in skilled manpower. The psychometric paradigm, with its static view of human ability and potential, became increasingly incompatible with the requirements of the economy; at the same time the arbitrary Norwood ideology became more and more dysfunctional. Secondly, on an intellectual level, the 1940s saw a gradual growth in attempts to move away from the tendency to view education and attainment predominantly in terms of individual psychology. Increasingly, concepts and explanations derived from sociology, social psychology and social history were invoked. Although it is possible to trace this development back to before 1940, the publication of Clarke (1940 and 1941), Richmond (1945) and Fleming (1944 and 1948) all represent very different but significant landmarks in this shift of emphasis, which did much to facilitate the rise of 'sociology of education' in Britain in the 1950s. These developments in educational thought in the 1940s owed almost everything to the quest for national efficiency during the Second World War and the post-war period of reconstruction.[36] However, Clarke, Richmond and Fleming did not actually reject the intelligence theory. They either ignored it or (as in the case of Fleming) stressed the need for a much broader, social perspective. However, the necessary paradigm-shift was not achieved easily. The fact that it ultimately needed a barrage of attacks to discredit the intelligence theory is a reflection of its hegemony and apparent impregnability at that time. Many years later Simon (1970, p. 239) wrote:

> It is not easy to recall the atmosphere of those days — how unquestioningly these ideas [psychometry] were accepted by the vast majority of educationists as well as psychologists, whatever their social outlook or political standpoint. Teachers had been brought up in these beliefs, embodied almost as a dogma in textbooks . . . The critique of intelligence testing, its theory, technology and educational outcome, could at that time only be undertaken from an independent standpoint, geared to seek out and challenge the basic, unstated assumptions of intelligence testing embedded in its technology.[37]

Simon (1953) does not merely attack the intelligence theory but also offers an alternative hypothesis to account for differential educational attainment — namely, that it is to a large extent an artefact of the education system itself and in particular is induced by classification and streaming. Of course, in 1953 he was primarily concerned with the artificial creation of success and failure by secondary selection itself and the practice of streaming in the junior school and in grammar schools. Yet his basic hypothesis extends to all forms of streaming, setting and stereotyping in schools, and in some respects he adumbrated the systematic application of the concept of the self-fulfilling prophecy to educational research.

In purely *practical* terms the publication of Simon (1953) did not, of course, destroy the intelligence theory[38] or put an end to the use of intelligence tests in schools. Nevertheless, by the late 1950s the theory had sustained a considerable battering and its hegemony was broken. (This did much to facilitate the campaign for comprehensive schools, for if the hegemony of the intelligence theory had not been broken, the only alternative open would have been to argue along the lines of Clarke (1941) – hardly a viable proposition in the 1950s.) More recently the concept of success and failure as artefacts of the education system has been carried much further. Whereas Simon (1953, 1967 and 1970) sought to identify within the education system particular features producing success and failure, a number of other education-alists (notably many of the deschoolers) have confused this highly specific concept with the view that school itself is an artefact doomed to failure. In its most extreme form, this hypothesis claims that because of their inevitably institutional character, any formal education system and any school are incapable of educating and that schools are morally, psychologically and socially corrupting. Logically enough, the deschoolers have called for the abolition of compulsory schooling. Less extreme variants of this hypothesis, for example Baratz and Baratz (1970) and Keddie (1972), have stressed the ethnocentric and allegedly middle-class values of the school and pleaded for an intense localisation of the curriculum to meet the needs of the community that any given school serves. Failure on the part of pupils is largely ascribed to attempts by the school to force irrelevant, inappropriate and intrinsically alienating values on the pupils. Despite its apparent radicalism, this line of reasoning points unambiguously to segregation along ethnic, social or neighbourhood lines – a point made by Chanan and Gilchrist (1974), Levitas (1976) and Simon (1976).

The verbal deficit theory, which is an attempt to account for the social distribution of educational attainment, was first advanced in the late 1950s in Britain and the early 1960s in the USA, though there had been forerunners. In the USA these included Templin (1957) and Schatzmann and Strauss (1955) and, in Britain, Nisbet (1953) as well as certain passages in various official reports from the interwar period, especially the Hadow Report (1931, p. 56) and more particularly the Newbolt Report (1921, pp. 59–69). When the verbal deficit theory was first advanced the intelligence theory was only gradually being called into question in the USA,[39] where it remained largely uncontroversial till 1969, and in Britain it still had not been dislodged decisively. This influenced the formulation of the verbal deficit theory. A frequently debated issue within psychometry had been the relative importance of heredity and environment, and to a considerable extent the verbal deficit theory, by stressing the pre-eminence of environment, unwittingly operated within much the same kind of framework as the intelligence theory. In particular, the theory embodies at a fundamental level highly deterministic concepts and tends to dichotomise the school population.

The term *verbal deficit* is used throughout this book in preference to the expression *verbal deprivation*. Of the two, the former is more neutral and merely suggests a shortfall, whereas the latter implies active depriving. Moreover, right up to and beyond the time when the verbal deficit theory was evolved in the late 1950s the terms *deprivation* and *deprived children* were often used in respect of children with clearly identifiable handicaps — often home backgrounds so grossly unsatisfactory as to require intervention by local authority social services departments, the NSPCC and the courts. For example, Ford (1955) uses the term *deprived child* in this sense. Although some proponents of the verbal deficit theory write about whole social strata as if they were 'social services cases' it is important to distinguish the verbal deficit theory from earlier concepts of deprivation. The purpose of this distinction is not to deny that to some extent the various concepts of deprivation have coalesced, but rather to focus on the specifically linguistic claims of the verbal deficit theory and those aspects of the theory that are novel and distinctive. Verbal deficit theories are generally presented not in isolation, but as the key element in more general theories of cultural deficit or deprivation or, in the case of Bernstein's collected papers on sociolinguistics, within the framework of much more ambitious sociological theories. This critique focuses primarily on the linguistic and sociolinguistic aspects of such theories, though other aspects are also considered where appropriate. The justification for this focus is that in nearly all the theories in question the concept of verbal deficit is central — to such an extent that if it can be shown to be misconceived or false, what then remains is generally of little significance. Thus the deficit theories will be criticised at what is at one and the same time their weakest point and their very core.

Notes

1.   For example, the Pimsleur Language Aptitude Battery which is some-times used to assess aptitude for learning a foreign language includes tests on 'previous performance in English, social studies, mathematics and science'

(James and Rouve, 1973, p. 146).

2.   Birchenough (1938, p. 1n) also stresses the need for flexibility in interpreting and defining the concept of elementary education: ' "Elementary
education" means the schooling which in any age represents the minimum
conscious needs of the community. In this sense it covers the provision for those
whose schooldays are circumscribed by the years of statutory attendance.'

3.   For a different typology of hypotheses used to explain differential
educational attainment, see Flude (1974).

4.   Runciman's story is set in a very poor part of London in the 1870s.

5.   See Simon (1960, pp. 47–50) for a fuller account of this.

6.   Quoted by Thomson (1929, p. 135).

7.   Stow (1836, p. 20).

8.   Stow (1836, pp. 20, 95–6, 112 and 172).

9.   Simon (1953, pp. 59–60) discusses this distinction in greater detail.

10.   See Pritchard (1963) and Rose (1979) for a detailed discussion of
nineteenth-century and early twentieth-century attitudes towards and treatment
of such children as fell into these and similar categories.

11.   It is interesting to note that when the second edition of *Hereditary
Genius* (1869) appeared in 1892 Galton expressed unease at the use of the word
genius in the title. Although Galton seems to have been unaware of it, the word
had undergone a change in meaning between the two dates. What had made
excellent sense in 1869 had become inappropriate by 1892. For a general discussion of the semantic history of this word, see Smith, L.P. (1924).

12.   A list of the manuals and other writings on education examined is
provided in Appendix 1.

13.   Birchenough (1938, pp. 98–9) gives a useful summary of contemporary
criticism of the Revised Code of 1862.

14.   Defending the Revised Code in the House of Commons, Lowe said:
'I cannot promise the House that this system will be an economical one, and I
cannot promise that it will be an efficient one, but I can promise that it shall
be either one or the other' (quoted by Curtis and Boultwood, 1964, p. 71).

15.   Sturt (1967, pp. 260–88) gives a vivid picture of the chaos caused in
many schools by the introduction of the Revised Code and this contrasts
sharply with the relatively neat model described by Simon. However, most of
Sturt's descriptions relate to the 1860s and early 1870s, and Simon states
explicitly that this model 'prevailed wherever it was possible'. Moreover, the
fact that the model proved difficult to operate in some schools does not alter
the assumptions underlying it. Finally, Collins (1887, p. 19), writing at the
time when the Revised Code was still in full operation, observes:

> The single classification consists in arranging the pupils in the same class
> for instruction in all the subjects taught in the school. This is the plan
> generally adopted, not only in elementary, but also middle-class and higher
> schools . . . As children in inspected schools must be presented for examin-
> ation in one standard for all subjects, it follows that in them the single
> classification must be adopted. With any other it would be exceedingly
> difficult to enable the class as a whole to fulfil the requirements of the
> Code.

16.   See Taylor (1842, p. iii).

17.   See Musgrove (1966, pp. 16–30, 55–62 and 69–72) for a fuller discussion of this phenomenon and its implications for education.

18.   Contrary to a widespread misconception, the 1870 Elementary
Education Act did not introduce universal compulsory schooling. As for

compulsion, the Act merely empowered the School Boards which it established
to pass bye-laws making school attendance compulsory between the ages of 5
and 10. Thus the Act was entirely permissive on the question of compulsion, and
it should be noted that School Boards were established only in those areas where
the number of existing elementary school places was deemed inadequate. As a
result, there were many parts of the country where there was no authority or
body legally competent to establish compulsion. This loop-hole was 'plugged' in
1876 when an Act was passed setting up School Attendance Committees for
areas with no School Boards, but it was not until 1880 that any positive
obligation was placed on either kind of body to make attendance compulsory
up to age 10. Beyond age 10 exemptions were permitted on a wide range of
grounds which varied enormously from one district to another. Children who
could not obtain any exemption had to attend school full-time up to age 13.
The progress towards universal full-time compulsion beyond age 10 was
extremely slow. Birchenough (1938, p. 123) notes:

> In 1893 the lowest age at which children might be wholly or partly excused
> from attendance at school was 11, and in 1899 this was raised to 12.
> Exception was, however, made for children in agricultural districts who
> under certain conditions might become half-timers at 11. In 1900 local
> authorities were *allowed* to raise the age of compulsory attendance from 13
> to 14. Within a few years no child under 14 years of age was *wholly* released
> from school *over more than half the country* unless he had passed the seventh
> standard. (Italics − JCBG)

In principle Standard VII could be passed at age 13 or even earlier, though this
was rare. Universal compulsory full-time education from 5 to 14 did not come
into effect until the relevant sections of the 1918 Education Act came into
operation in 1922. The whole history of compulsory education, which had
started for some children (at least in principle) with the Health and Morals of
Apprentices Act (1802) provides an extreme example of piecemeal legislation
and gradualism.

19. See Lowndes (1969, p. 62). On the question of ambiguities in the 1870
Act, see Barlow and Macan (1903, pp. 5−8 and 103) and Birchenough (1938,
p. 134).

20. At the beginning of this period, for example, Sir John Gorst, who was in
effect the Minister responsible for education from 1895 to 1902 wrote:

> While primary instruction should be provided for, and even enforced upon
> all, advanced instruction is for the few. It is in the interest of the common-
> wealth at large that every boy and girl showing capacities above the
> average should be caught and given the best opportunities for developing
> these capacities. It is not in its interest to scatter broadcast a huge system
> of higher instruction for anyone who chooses to take advantage of it,
> however unfit to receive it. (Quoted by Simon 1965, p. 238)

Sir Robert Morant, Permanent Secretary at the Board of Education (1902−11),
included a passage in a similar vein in the Code for Public Elementary Schools,
issued in 1904:

> It will be an important though subsidiary object of the School to discover
> individual children who show promise of exceptional capacity, and to
> develop their special gifts (so far as this can be done without sacrificing the
> interests of the majority of the children), so that they may be qualified to

pass at the proper age into Secondary Schools . . . (Quoted in the Board of
Education's *Handbook of Suggestions* . . . , 1937, p. 10)

The persistence of this kind of mentality (in various different forms) is well
illustrated by the fact that as late as 1963 the Minister of Education, Sir Edward
Boyle, found it necessary to appeal for a 'change of heart' even towards pupils
of average ability. In the Foreword to the Newsom Report (1963, p. iv) he
wrote:

> . . . there is above all a need for new modes of thought, and a change of
> heart, on the part of the community as a whole. We who are professionally
> and constitutionally concerned with the work of the schools cannot hope
> to discover the true needs of these pupils, and the best means of meeting
> them, without the backing of widely informed public opinion.

He goes on to express his hope that there 'will be a general raising of sights in
our attitudes towards these pupils', referring to children aged 13 to 16 of average
and less than average ability.
   21. It is not possible to give a detailed exposition of the (British) Herbartian
School here. Those who are interested in following up the subject will find a
useful outline in Selleck (1968, pp. 227–72). They may also find it useful to
read some of the major works by the Herbartians themselves, in particular
Adams (1897), Dodd (1906) and Welton (1915).
   22. For a useful contemporary account of the Eugenics Movement of 1901–
14 see Schuster (1913), who was a prominent member of the movement. For a
recent account, see Searle (1976).
   23. This process is described in detail by Simon (1960, pp. 299–335).
Scott-Giles and Slater (1966, pp. 71–82), though primarily concerned with the
history of one particular institution, provide a brief but valuable account of one
of the most ambitious and complex schemes executed during this period,
namely the complete and simultaneous reorganisation of no less than five
endowed institutions (two schools and three 'hospitals') in the City of
Westminster. Their account also gives a fair indication of the extent of local and
even national hostility aroused by the activities of the Endowed Schools
Commissioners at the time (1869–74).
   24. See the *Report of the Departmental Committee on Scholarships and
Free Places* (1920, pp. 35–7 and 64–8) and Tawney (ed., 1922, pp. 35–49).
   25. These statistics are taken from the *Board of Education Annual Reports*
(and *Statistics*) as reproduced in Simon (1974, pp. 363–5).
   26. Sutherland (1977, pp. 144–53) outlines the actual spread of the use of
group intelligence tests for the purposes of secondary selection. They were
first used for this purpose in Bradford in 1919.
   27. Hayward (1912, pp. 232–3) makes a jibe about intelligence testing, but
later in the same book (pp. 292–3) writes:

> Of human abilities, as if they were unimportant, we keep no record.
> Administrative committees appoint men clumsily on the basis of a few
> testimonials, prejudices and impressions, while all the time there should
> exist, in the national archives, the records of the candidate's school and
> after school career, bearing clear witness to general or specific ability.
>   We are driven, therefore, to the recommendation of a system of school
> examinations for testing native ability in the pupil . . .

This amounted to nothing less than a complete volte-face. In fact, this kind of record-keeping was one of the objects for which the Eugenics Movement was campaigning at the time.

28. See Adams (1897, pp. 81–106 and 1928, pp. 60–91).

29. See Welton (1915, pp. 13–15).

30. See, for example, McPherson (1949) and the more general debate on the subject in Vols. 4 and 5 (New Series) of the *Modern Quarterly*.

31. The main exchanges between Lippmann and Terman, covering the period 1921–3, are reprinted with a brief introduction in Block and Dworkin (eds., 1976, pp. 1–44).

32. The concept of 'social inheritance' was not new and had already been discussed in some detail by Sully (1897, pp. 79–92).

33. Clarke (1941, pp. 106–7).

34. This manual was reprinted six times between 1928 and 1937.

35. *Secondary Education. A Report of the Advisory Council on Education in Scotland* (1947).

36. The spirit of 'national reconstruction' in these publications is epitomised in the dedication of Fleming (1944) which reads:

To Managers in Business
To Foremen in Factories
To Leaders in Clubs
To Parents in Homes
To Husbands. To Wives
To Sisters. To Brothers
To All who have Tried to Educate even on one Day.

37. The 'independent standpoint' referred to is Marxism. Brian and Joan Simon also had the additional advantage of being aware of the Soviet decree of 1936.

38. Uncritical acceptance of the intelligence theory remained remarkably persistent. In 1962 the journal *Sixth Form Opinion*, most of whose editors and contributors came from HMC (and comparable girls') schools, undertook a survey of political attitudes among its readers. These were published in *Sixth Form Opinion*, 5 (pp. 27–30), which came out early in 1963. Of the self-selecting sample which replied, 46 per cent of the boys and 38 per cent of the girls believed that 'People must pass an intelligence test before holding the right to vote'. The article containing the results of the survey is entitled 'If I were an M.P.', and the editor, Dyan Wade (1963, p. 27) begins the article with the remark 'Thank heaven you're not'. She continues: 'With bitter disappointment I realize that our generation is to be like hundreds of previous generations accepting all that it is told . . .'.

39. See Hunt (1961).

2 'CLASSICAL' VERBAL DEFICIT THEORY

There is no generally agreed definition of what constitutes a verbal deficit theory. In the absence of a ready-made yardstick of this kind it is not surprising that there is sometimes disagreement as to whether a theory is or is not a verbal deficit theory.[1] But it is noteworthy that disagreements of this kind seem to have arisen only in the late 1960s when verbal deficit (together with the concept of compensatory education) first became something of a 'dirty word' among some sociolinguists and others, and when Bernstein (1969) made a vigorous attempt to dissociate his work from the theory. As long as verbal deficit theories remained respectable, and indeed fashionable, there seems to have been no such disagreement; but, on the other hand, no serious attempt at definition was made at that stage, presumably because the concept was either thought to be clear or simply taken for granted. The latter possibility would suggest that, far from being new, the verbal deficit theory amounted at least initially to little more than a formalisation of attitudes already prevalent on language, social class and educational attainment. It is possible to define the concept of verbal deficit in purely formalistic terms, but such definitions amount to little more than a statement to the effect that some varieties of language are regarded by some people as intrinsically inferior to an implicit or explicit norm.[2] Although this is a prerequisite for any verbal deficit theory it is inadequate as a definition since it divorces the concept of verbal deficit from its prime function as a hypothesis seeking to account for differential educational attainment and its uneven distribution within society. There is nothing new about the mere fact that the varieties of language generally used by the working classes are widely regarded as substandard. Thus a narrow, formalistic definition runs the risk of ignoring the specific social and historical function of verbal deficit theories.

In view of the fact that Bernstein's attempt to dissociate his own work from the verbal deficit theory has further complicated the concept of verbal deficit itself, the only way to proceed towards a definition is to begin by examining a corpus of writings whose status as verbal deficit theories has not seriously been called into question, and which for that reason may aptly be referred to as examples of *classical* verbal deficit theory. By examining these works critically it will be possible to elucidate the essential features of the classical theory, proceed from there to a definition and subsequently examine variants of the theory. (Bernstein's sociolinguistic work is so important in this field, and also so controversial, that it is treated separately.) The following are taken to constitute a fair and significant sample of classical verbal deficit theory: Bereiter and Engelmann (1966), Bereiter *et al.* (1966), Deutsch *et al.* (1967), Gahagan and Gahagan (1970), Jensen (1968), Riessmann (1962) and the material from the Walsall Seminar organised in 1968 under the auspices of the National Association for the Teaching of English, reproduced by Creber (1972, pp. 76–8).

All these writings either propose or assume the existence of two very broad, generalised types of language or language-use which may conveniently be referred to as the *high variety* and the *low variety*, though the theorists themselves do not use these terms. (In this chapter the terms *high* and *low* are used in this specific sense, which does not correspond to the sense in which they are normally used in socio-linguistics, for example Ferguson (1959).) The theorists suggest that the former is normally used, at least in the classroom, by teachers and successful pupils and, more generally, they associate it with the middle classes. The low variety is seen in the corpus as characteristic of pupils who fail and, again more generally, it is associated with the working classes and certain ethnic minority groups. What actually are these two varieties of language? On this important question all the works in the corpus are curiously reticent, inexplicit and in some cases also very confused. Riessmann (1962, pp. 74–80) is clearer than most, though to a large extent he merely cites the work of others. In particular, he accepts the characteristics of *public* and *formal language* given by Bernstein (1959). He also cites the use of casual or informal vocabulary as characteristic of the language of the deprived, and also quotes some material from an unpublished report by Deutsch. The general gist of the report is that deprived children understand more than they speak and have a considerable facility for phantasy, spontaneity and the use of descriptive adjectives. Riessmann (1962, p. 77) also comments on the behaviour of deprived children in word-association tests, noting that the responses are often 'less conventional, more unusual, original and independent' and adding that these children 'seem to be more flexible and visual with language'. All this, though interesting, is far too fragmentary to amount to an adequate characteris-ation of an identifiable variety of language. Few of the other writings in the corpus even go into the desultory detail provided by Riessmann. Deutsch *et al.* (1967) seem to assume that the low variety can be identified by low scores on various kinds of vocabulary tests. But in most of the works in the corpus it is simply taken for granted that there exist two distinct varieties of language — one vastly inferior to the other — and that any researcher can tell without difficulty which variety any particular child speaks.

This reticence on the subject of the actual characteristics of the two varieties is remarkable and at the same time very revealing. The writings in the corpus are concerned with ways of helping children suffering from supposed verbal (and other) deficits. A prerequisite for giving help of this kind is some adequate means of identifying those who actually need it, and without a clear linguistic description of the two varieties such identification is impossible. However, in both the USA and Britain some children have been given compensatory language teaching or have participated in 'verbal enrichment' programmes. (This kind of teaching is concerned with developing the spoken language and should not be confused with remedial teaching in basic literacy.) Since none of the proponents of the verbal deficit hypothesis has yet succeeded in providing adequate descriptions of the two varieties, one can only assume that those children who have been given compensatory language teaching have been selected either on the basis of non-linguistic or at best folk-linguistic criteria. The deficit theorists generally write about the high and low varieties as if they were newly discovered varieties of speech recently identified by educational psychologists and some sociologists. The possibility that this dichotomous model might to a large extent coincide with varieties of speech widely held in high and low esteem in society in general, and more particularly in the classroom, does not seem to have occurred to them. Their reticence on what is, after all, presented as an important discovery arouses precisely this suspicion, and those rare instances where the two varieties are described in the corpus tend to confirm that the deficit theorists are operating primarily with folk-linguistic premises which have been left unquestioned. For example, Bereiter *et al.* (1966, p. 121) frown on pupils who reply to the question 'Where is the squirrel?' by saying 'In the tree' rather than 'The squirrel is in the tree.' Riessmann (1962, p. 75) writes: 'The communication of the deprived is famous for its use of imaginative nicknames and shortenings — the British "never-never" for installment buying, "telly" for TV, "pub" for bar or public place [sic].'

Even more revealing is the fact that Riessmann (1962, p. 75) quotes,

with obvious sympathy, some of the characteristics given by Bernstein
(1959, pp. 42–3 and 43n3) for *public* and *formal language*. Of the
former he cites *inter alia* 'short, grammatically simple, often unfinished
sentences . . . ' and for the latter 'Accurate order and syntax regulate
what is said . . . '. There is nothing original about any of this. Most
readers aged 30+, and many younger ones, will be only too familiar
from their own schooldays with the traditional preoccupation with
complete-sentence answers, 'correct grammar' and many teachers'
horror of 'slang'. Folk-linguistic attitudes are based on the connotations
of various words, linguistic forms, accents and dialects, and especially
on popular, stereotyped attitudes towards the speakers of different
varieties of language; for this reason they mingle and merge with non-
linguistic cultural value-judgements. Indeed, many folk-linguistic
attitudes are commonly expressed in moral or quasi-moral terms, for
example: *bad grammar, slovenly speech, sloppy pronunciation*, and
foul language. In verbal deficit theories, too, there is a strong
tendency for value-judgements on speech to go hand in hand with
cultural, moral and quasi-moral judgements. A striking example of
this is provided in the material from the Walsall Seminar quoted by
Creber (1972). A study group at the seminar drew up a list of the
'personal characteristics and language habits of the disadvantaged'
(Creber 1972, p. 76). The list of language habits (*not* personal
characteristics) reads as follows:

Language habits
1. Speaks in a very limited vocabulary.
2. Reproduces sounds inaccurately.
3. Misnames objects or omits naming them.
4. Speaks haltingly without physical defect.
5. Often speaks in monotone.
6. Indiscriminate in both noisy and quiet responses.
7. Seldom or never asks questions.
8. Constantly uses present tense.
9. Seldom uses modifiers.
10. Cause and effect relationships absent in speech.
11. Rarely engages in dialogue with adults.
12. Talks almost exclusively about things.
13. Avoids situations which require words.
14. Tells transparent lies.
15. Distrusts vocal people, especially those who use 'big' words.
16. Exhibits too ready agreement.

17. Cannot easily transfer abstracted information into concrete usage.
18. Unable to vary language with situation.
19. Reluctant to move from oral to written language. (Quoted by Creber, 1972, p. 77)

What, one wonders, made 'tells transparent lies' appear to the study group to be typical of the 'language habits of the disadvantaged': transparency or dishonesty? Would they prefer clever and effective deceit, or were they in an off-guard moment saying that they regard lower working-class children as liars? In fact, moral value-judgements on those with whom the high and low varieties are associated (namely the middle and lower working classes respectively) abound in the corpus. Gahagan and Gahagan (1970, p. 13), for example, provide an apotheosis of the intelligentsia that would not be easy to rival:

> Consider a five-year-old boy whose parents are both teachers. His parents will have observed his pleasure in making logical distinctions, or symmetrical patterns, or perhaps simply his musical ability and his disinterest in reading. They will have already noted in considerable detail his clearly intellectual performance. They will have made available by conversation and by the provision of carefully designed toys and so on an opportunity for him to develop his intellectual ability. And they will be in a degree of concordance about his interests. Consider on the other hand a five-year-old boy whose mother is a housewife and whose father is a docker . . .

Occasionally, the value-judgements almost run riot. Jensen (1968, p. 116) rejects notions of 'good' and 'bad' English and goes on to suggest something much more drastic:

> . . . language in the lower class is not as flexible a means of communication as in the middle class. It is not as readily adapted to the subtleties of the particular situation, but consists more of a relatively small repertoire of stereotyped phrases and expressions which are used rather loosely without much effort to achieve a subtle correspondence between perception and verbal expression. Much of lower-class language consists of a kind of incidental 'emotional' accompaniment to action here and now. In contrast, middle-class language, rather than being a mere accompaniment to ongoing activity, serves more to represent things and events not

immediately present. (1968, pp. 118–19)

These value-judgements are highly significant. First, they support the
hypothesis that under the guise of generalisations and judgements
about language, judgement is in fact being passed on speakers – not
speech. Secondly, they also suggest equally strongly that very little
attention is actually being given to speech: instead, people whose life-
styles are deemed in some sense 'low' are unthinkingly and automatically assumed to have at their disposal only the low variety of
language.[3] Gahagan and Gahagan (1970) describe in considerable
detail a compensatory language education programme which they
devised and which they subsequently tested in the East End of
London. When embarking on the experimental stage they administered
verbal IQ tests to the children involved. They discovered that the
'working-class sample obtained a mean standardised score of 101.02'
and go on to comment: 'we found ourselves with a sample of 5 year
old working-class children whose verbal and non-verbal ability was
distributed in the same way as that of the general population' (1970,
pp. 24–5). Yet these children were treated as suitable candidates
for compensatory language teaching.[4] It is tempting to conclude
that the Gahagans had decided in advance that because these children
lived in the East End of London they jolly well needed to have their
language improved, despite the normality of the test scores.
Significantly, Little and Smith (1971, p. 36), when discussing the
conceptual weaknesses of many of the assumptions underlying compensatory education, observe: 'In one sense, everybody knows
which groups are being referred to when phrases such as "the
underprivileged", "the deprived" or "the disadvantaged" are used.'

The contention that very little attention is paid to speech is
borne out by the 'giant word' hypothesis which appears in
Bereiter and Engelmann (1966, pp. 34–7) and Gahagan and
Gahagan (1970, p. 14). This seems to have been invented by Bereiter
and Engelmann and consists of the notion that lower working-class
children speak in invariant phrases consisting of whole words. It is
instructive to examine the actual examples of 'giant words' given
by these authors:

	Standard or near-standard
Examples given	*adult equivalent*
(1) He bih daw	He's a big dog
(2) Uai-ga-na-ju	I ain't go no juice

(3) Da-re-truh	That's a red truck
(4) Re-ih-bu	Read me the book
(5) Two pluh wunic'k three	Two plus one equals three
(6) wipeyerfeetorI'lltellyerdad	Wipe your feet or I'll tell your dad

(The last example is taken from Gahagan and Gahagan (1970, p. 14), the others from Bereiter and Engelmann (1966, pp. 34—7)).

Before any of these examples is discussed individually three points should be noted. First, these 'examples' seem to have been invented by the authors. Bereiter and Engelmann (1966, p. 34) state that 'the [sic] deprived child says "He bih daw" ' — not that a child actually said it. A little later they say that 'The culturally deprived child . . . would probably start off with some amalgam like "re-ih-bu" . . .' Secondly, Bereiter et al. (1966, p. 114) claim that 'The pronunciation of several of the children was so substandard that, when they did talk, the teachers had no notion of what they were saying.' This kind of statement does nothing to inspire confidence in the ability or willingness of either Bereiter et al. or Bereiter and Engelmann to understand what these children said! Thirdly, Houston (1971) has described some of the pitfalls facing those who, without training in dialectology or phonetics, try to transcribe non-standard speech and demonstrates that Bereiter and Engelmann have fallen into some of these traps.[5] For all these reasons, it would be wrong to treat the 'examples' as transcriptions: they represent merely the kind of speech that the authors associate with the children with whom they were concerned.

Superficially, some of the 'examples' look the kind of utterances commonly produced by children aged about two years. However, since the children that Bereiter and Engelmann are writing about were about four years old, even these invented 'examples' deserve closer scrutiny. 'Examples' (1) to (4) seem to lack all consonants in word-final position. Since the children were Negroes the explanation is relatively simple. Discussing the Sandhi rules of Child Black English, Houston (1971, pp. 242—3) notes that 'since Child Black English does tend to eliminate many final consonants present in standard English, the former often sounds as though it has numerous elisions or omissions of phonological items'. As for the 'omissions' of the copula in (1) and (3), Black English Vernacular (BEV) often simply does not have a copular in such contexts. In this respect BEV is by no means unique: for example, in Russian there is normally no copula in statements in the present tense, and Latin mottos rarely contain a copula, either. One cannot draw any conclusions, on the basis of the presence or absence of the copula in a language or dialect, about its speakers' abilities to reason. In purely distributional terms the frequent absence of the copula in BEV is described by Labov *et al.* (1968, I, p. 185) as follows, and this formulation covers (1) and (3): 'One general principle holds without exception: wherever SE [= Standard English] can contract, NNE [= Negro speech] can delete *is* and *are*, and vice-versa; wherever SE cannot contract, NNE cannot delete *is* and *are*, and vice-versa.'

This leaves the omitted articles in (1), (3) and (4) as the only un-explained phenomenon in (1) to (4). 'Example' (5) represents one of the early attempts of a four-year-old child to use the terminology of mathematics; no-one should be surprised if the unfamiliar terms *plus* and *equals* cause some initial difficulty, especially when used in frozen, ritualistic, classroom recitations, yet it none the less conforms to the criteria given by Houston. As for the last 'example', it ought to go down as a joke. The Gahagans have taken a perfectly normal English sentence, written it as one word, changed *your* to *yer* in a rather coy attempt to add a little local colour, and have declared the result a giant word. Apparently, they wish to imply that *feet* could not be replaced by *hands*, nor *dad* by *mum*.

The proponents of the 'giant word' hypothesis overlook the fact that speech is a continuum, interrupted by pauses, hesitations, other speakers and extraneous factors: people do not solemnly pause between each word, even when dictating. Thus if people claim to hear 'giant words' this can only be attributed to the way the hearer perceives the continuum. In practice, this kind of perception generally arises only when people are confronted with a language or dialect that they do not understand well or at all. The 'giant word syndrome', far from being a feature of the speech of some children, is a perceptual problem peculiar to a handful of psychologists. The general tenor of the writings concerned suggests that this problem arises from contempt for the children whom these people want to help rather than actual inability to understand. Like some nationalistic govern-ments which try to suppress minority languages, Bereiter *et al.* (1966, pp. 112–13) seem reluctant to accord the speech that they so dislike the status of language at all[6] and propose nothing less than its systematic eradiction 'at least in school settings':

It seems to have been taken for granted by other educators that one

must begin by encouraging the child to make the fullest possible use
of the language he already possesses before one may set about improving it. Our estimation of the language of culturally deprived
children agrees, however, with that of Bernstein, who maintains
that this language is not merely an underdeveloped version of
standard English, but is a basically non-logical mode of expressive
behavior which lacks the formal properties necessary for the
organization of thought. From this point of view, the goal of
language training for the culturally deprived could be seen as not
that of improving the child's language but rather that of teaching
him a different language which would hopefully replace the first
one, at least in school settings. The two languages share lexical
elements and these we made use of, but apart from this we pro-
ceeded much as if the children had no language at all.

Thus it is largely on the basis of unexamined folk-linguistic assumptions[7]
that classical verbal deficit theory seeks to account for differential
educational attainment and its distribution in society. Of course, as
noted in the final paragraph of Chapter 1, the theory does not attempt
to explain these phenomena on the basis of language alone, but the
role assigned to language is crucial. Riessmann (1962, p. 80), who
may be regarded as one of the founding-fathers of the theory
in the USA, states: 'Despite various sources of latent creativity, underprivileged children apparently do not realize their potential because
of formal language deficiencies. This is their Achilles heel.' It has long
been accepted that there exists some relationship between linguistic
and cognitive development in the child, though the precise nature of
the relationship has been the subject of much uncertainty and debate.[8]
Before the rise of classical verbal deficit theory the relationship was
generally discussed in terms of normal, abnormal and retarded
linguistic and cognitive development. What is essentially new in
classical verbal deficit theory is the assumption that habitual or
exclusive use of the low variety of language amounts in itself to
abnormal or retarded linguistic development. The theory goes on to
assume that this automatically produces a considerable measure of
cognitive deficit, as if the relationship between linguistic and cognitive
development was relatively unproblematical. However, the theory
fails to provide anything approaching adequate recognition criteria for
the high and low varieties of language with which it operates. Thus
in practice the deficit theorists take it largely for granted that certain
categories of children suffer from cognitive deficiencies, and these

children are identified on the basis of non-standard dialects which are assumed to be inherently substandard. In this way the linguistic dimension of classical verbal deficit serves in practice (though not in theory) as a convenient vehicle for the expression of the view that the 'lower orders' of society suffer from grave cognitive defects which impair their educability. Although some telling gaffes have already been noted in this chapter the theorists themselves are generally reluctant to express themselves in such terms and in many cases may well be unaware of the full implications of their reasoning and their compensatory education programmes.

When linguists like Labov, Stubbs and Trudgill make use of a standard/non-standard dichotomy, they do so in order to facilitate the discussion of different varieties of the language and, above all, of social attitudes towards these varieties, their uses and their speakers. Similarly, Ferguson (1959), when writing about high and low varieties of language, is concerned with the contexts in which the two varieties are used and for which they are considered appropriate. With these writers the dichotomy is conceived of in strictly sociological and linguistic terms. In classical verbal deficit theory, however, the dichotomy is seen primarily in psychological and folk-linguistic terms: the high variety contains some x-formula ensuring success at school, and the low variety contains a y-formula which steers pupils inexorably towards failure. This hypothesis, or at least the second part of it, is central to the theory.

The only way in which one can attempt to support this hypothesis is by stressing the allegedly harmful cognitive effects of the low variety — and this is precisely what verbal deficit theories do. Folk-linguistics of the pseudo-academic rather than the popular kind has often held that some varieties of language and some languages are more logical than others. In general, the higher the prestige-rating of a language, the greater the degree of logic claimed for it. Latin and often French, too, are sometimes said to be more logical than English and German, and among English dialects, the standard dialect is often said to be more logical than non-standard dialects.[9] A broadly similar view is also to be found in classical verbal deficit theory where it is con-joined to a concept of linguistic determinism — the view that one's thinking is constrained or even largely determined by one's language. There is some disagreement and confusion as to whether the low variety is necessarily illogical, or not used logically, but this merely reflects the authors' failure to give much serious thought to linguistic questions. The hypothesis put forward is that the low variety is, in effect, illogical speech, and that therefore its speakers cannot develop normally from a cognitive point of view and cannot think logically or on an abstract level.

Despite occasional suggestions that the issue is partly a matter of experience in using language for a wide range of different purposes, it is remarkable that no serious attempt is made to work out exactly what features of the low variety of speech give rise to exactly what kinds of cognitive problems. Instead, the reader is offered a series of *ex cathedra* pronouncements. This comes across with almost disarming naivety in Gahagan and Gahagan (1970, p. 4).

> We do believe that the development of intelligence and the acquisition of knowledge are to a large extent dependent on our starting off with reasonable verbal resources.
>
> We do believe that this spiral of disadvantagement is based on inadequate language early in life.

By treating the relationship between speech and cognitive development as an article of faith, verbal deficit theories mystify the whole area of language, social class and education. Without this kind of mystification it would be quite impossible to insinuate that a low variety of speech has a y-formula which predestines pupils to failure or, to use the familiar slogan, that 'educational failure is linguistic failure'. Rosen (1974, pp. 2–3) notes that the concept of verbal deficit has largely replaced that of the IQ. Like the IQ, the y-formula (and, of course, the x-formula of the high variety of speech) is largely undefined and undefinable, defies rational and empirical scrutiny and is credited with immense explanatory power.

Some readers may be surprised that the welter of statistical data often cited as supportive evidence or even proof of the classical verbal deficit theory has been left out of account in this analysis. The reasons for this are threefold:

1. The bulk of the data consist of IQ test scores (verbal and non-verbal). Verbal IQ tests generally consist of vocabulary tests in the sense that the problems test – or appear to test – either knowledge of the meanings of individual words or the subject's total stock of words (by means of various sampling procedures), and there is no evidence to support the implicit contention that there exists any relationship between such test scores and facility in expressing oneself.[10] One does not have to be a linguist to appreciate that language does not consist of

vocabulary alone. It consists even less in the ability to provide such answers to vocabulary tests as the psychologists devising the tests happen to be willing to accept as correct![11] Furthermore, one is entitled to ask: What is this thing glorying in the name of *verbal intelligence*? Even Eysenck (1962, p. 10 and 1971, pp. 49–54) in effect reluctantly admits that psychologists cannot say what intelligence *is*. If intelligence itself is an obscure essence, then varieties of it must be equally if not more so.

2. All the data concerned ignore most of the various complex constraints of the test situation.

3. Most of the remaining data are concerned with mother-child interaction in test situations. Again, the inherent situational constraints are ignored.[12] Moreover, the very preoccupation of the deficit theorists with mother-child interaction is normative in character and is yet another reflection of their belief that virtually every aspect of the culture of the 'lower orders' is deleterious and dysfunctional. At the same time this can be interpreted as a form of special pleading: if the lower working-class mother's child-rearing practices can be shown to be harmful, then intervention (by qualified psychologists and educationalists) is not only justified but virtuous. It is curious, yet noteworthy, that when discussing the allegedly harmful home-upbringing of lower working-class children the deficit theorists write as if the rest of society subscribed to an undisputed orthodoxy as to what constitutes sound child-rearing practices.

It is now possible to provide a summary of the essential tenets of classical verbal deficit theory and proceed to a definition. The theory presupposes that differential educational attainment can largely be accounted for by means of the following assumptions:

1. That speech falls into two broad categories — a generalised high and a generalised low variety — and that the former is intrinsically superior to the latter.

2. That both varieties are readily recognisable, either intuitively or on the basis of verbal IQ tests, and that linguistic definitions are superfluous.

3. That the high variety is spoken by those pupils who are successful

at school, while the majority of those who fail at school can speak only the low variety.

4. That the high variety contains the necessary ingredients for normal cognitive development and hence academic success, while the low variety lacks precisely these characteristics and thus hampers cognitive development and so leads to academic failure.

In the classical theory two further tenets account for the social distribution of educational attainment:

5. That *all* lower working-class children (and adults (?)) and those belonging to most non-white ethnic minority groups speak only the low variety.

6. That *only* lower working-class children (and adults (?)) and those belonging to most non-white ethnic minority groups habitually use the low variety at home and in school.

These tenets can be simplified in the form of a definition: *A verbal deficit theory is any hypothesis that (i) seeks to explain differential educational attainment to any significant degree in terms of the intrinsic nature of two fundamentally different varieties of language used by schoolchildren, both at the commencement of their school careers and subsequently; and (ii) seeks to explain the unequal social distribution of educational attainment in terms of which social groups are deemed to speak one of the two varieties rather than the other.*
Nowhere in the classical verbal deficit theory are these tenets stated together explicitly, nor does the theory offer any definition of the kind presented here. In many writings in the corpus there is a strange ambivalence as to whether children allegedly suffering from a verbal deficit lack normal human language altogether, or whether they merely possess a vernacular that the deficit theorists regard as educationally dysfunctional. This ambivalence is further compounded by a tendency in some cases to see certain varieties of language as positively dangerous. In this respect there are highly significant echoes of the Newbolt Report (1921, pp. 59–60):

The great difficulty of teachers in Elementary Schools in many districts is that they have to fight against the powerful influence of evil habits of speech contracted in home and street. The teachers' struggle is thus not with ignorance but with a perverted power . . .

Plainly, then the first and chief duty of the Elementary School is to give its pupils speech — to make them articulate and civilised human beings, able to communicate themselves in speech and writing, and able to receive the communication of others. It must be remembered that children, until they can readily receive such communication, are entirely cut off from the life and thought and experience of the race embodied in human words. Indeed, until they have been given civilised speech it is useless to talk of continuing their education, for, in a real sense, their education has not begun.

Thanks to the absence here of any psychological, sociological or linguistic jargon, and the open reliance on folk-linguistics and on sheer class prejudice, this passage encapsulates most of the main assumptions of classical verbal deficit theory much more explicitly than any of the writings in the corpus, and at the same time serves to show how little of the theory is in any real sense new. One must of course make due allowance for the fact that American educationalists cannot reasonably be expected to be aware of the Newbolt Report, but similar attitudes were prevalent in the USA at that time and, at least to some extent, subsequently.

In this chapter an attempt has been made to work out and formulate the underlying assumptions in classical verbal deficit theory. In order to carry out this essential and long overdue analysis it has been necessary to make a number of criticisms, if only because there is no other way of elucidating assumptions which are usually taken so much for granted in the classical theory that they generally pass unquestioned and often unstated.

But before concluding this chapter a few comments must be made on the subject of language, thought and cognitive development, if only because the foregoing discussion may have given rise to the impression that language is irrelevant to cognitive processes and their development. Probably no linguist would deny that language plays a significant role in many cognitive processes — in particular, categorisation, planning, self-monitoring and abstract reasoning. The general case, argued for example by Vygotsky (1962) and demonstrated by Luria and Yudovich (1959), is hardly open to serious doubt, provided that due allowance is made for the fact that not all cognitive processes are necessarily or entirely based on language. Thus if a child literally had no language, normal cognitive development would be impossible. However, Labov *et al.* (1968) and Labov (1969) have successfully dispelled the myth of the non-verbal child (with the obvious exception of genuinely abnormal or pathological cases).

What linguists do not accept are notions that any one variety of speech is intrinsically superior to another for the purposes of cognitive development. This notion has already been discussed and exposed as a purely social value-judgement on non-standard dialects and their speakers. If one dialect were superior in cognitive terms to another, then the same would be true in an even more striking form in respect of differences between languages, and there is no evidence that speakers of any particular language are cognitively more developed by virtue of their language than speakers of any other language. Admittedly, some cultures are in some senses more developed than others, but this can be explained perfectly adequately on social, economic, historical and geographical grounds without invoking language at all. It is a truism that the grammars of all languages are immensely complex, and that any language can adopt or create new lexical items as and when conditions require.

The other proposition (implicit in the classical verbal deficit theory) which modern linguistics does not seriously entertain is that of *linguistic determinism* — the notion that the specific nature of one's perception, categorisation and reasoning is governed by one's particular native dialect or language. The last linguist of any note to advance a theory of this kind was Benjamin Lee Whorf (1897–1941) who for a time worked in collaboration with Edward Sapir (1884–1939), with whose views on linguistic determinism he had much in common. Some deficit theorists appeal to 'the Whorfian hypothesis', but there is disagreement among linguists as to what this hypothesis actually is.[13] In fact, Whorf's papers propose an unambiguously deterministic theory.[14] For example, Whorf (1940a, pp. 212–13) states:

> . . . the background linguistic system (in other words, the grammar) of each language is not merely a reproducing instrument for voicing ideas but rather is itself the shaper of ideas, the program and guide for the individual's mental activity, for his analysis of impressions, for his synthesis of his mental stock in trade. Formulation of ideas is not an independent process, strictly rational in the old sense, but is part of a particular grammar, and differs, from slightly to greatly, between different grammars.

Such statements cannot be tested. The whole issue is, as Stubbs

(1980, p. 107) notes, condemned to 'irremediable circularity', because: 'Whorf argues that the grammatical structure of a speaker's language influences thought; but it is difficult to see how evidence of this could be obtained, since evidence of what someone thinks can only be obtained via language.'

The circularity goes even further than this. If, as Whorf suggests, grammars play a central role in the formulation of ideas and even of reason itself, and if, as Whorf (1940b, p. 221) claims, 'users of markedly different grammars are . . . not equivalent as observers of the world but must arrive at somewhat different views of the world', then it is open to question how one could learn a foreign language sufficiently well to make claims of this kind at all. Whorf's view of language is static and implies a static view of society. If speakers were, psychologically and philosophically, virtual prisoners of the grammars of their native languages it is very difficult to see how any society could ever undergo radical change; for, according to Whorf's view, the far-reaching changes in social psychology, culture, political and economic outlook which accompany such changes would scarcely be possible since the language(s) spoken in the society concerned would presumably be unable to accommodate the necessary conceptual changes.[15] Like most proponents of theories of linguistic determinism, Whorf does not distinguish adequately between language and culture. For example, Whorf (1942, p. 252) claims:

> And every language is a vast pattern-system, different from others, in which are culturally ordained the forms and categories by which the personality not only communicates, but also analyzes nature, notices or neglects types of relationship and phenomena, channels his reasoning, and builds the house of his consciousness.

In some versions of the verbal deficit theory Whorfian metaphysics serve as a convenient device for two functions. First, they mystify relationships between varieties of language and cognitive development. Secondly, since the distinction between language (or dialect) and culture is blurred, value-judgements on population-groups become masked. The deficit theorist can judge varieties of language or lifestyles or both, without necessarily passing explicit judgements on social groups or strata as such, though (as noted) judgements of this latter kind are rarely avoided altogether. However, they are less frequent, and often less obvious, than would be the case if the theory did not incorporate notions of linguistic determinism.

Notes

1. For a discussion of this problem see Stubbs (1980, pp. 143–50).
2. The following is an example of a purely formal definition, based on that given in Gordon (1976b, p. 32):

1. The speech of a speaker A or a group of speakers X is compared either explicitly or implicitly with a norm N. The comparison may relate to the speech of A or X either in a given context, or in contexts deemed comparable, or in a range of contexts, or generally. N may be either the speech of another speaker or group of speakers, or it may be a model in the mind of the investigator.

2. The comparison reveals differences between the speech of A and/or X on the one hand and N on the other. The differences may be in any one or more of the following areas: phonetics, phonology, morphology, syntax, semantics, register.

3. At least some of the differences are seen as *inadequacies* in the speech of A and/or X.

3. See Trudgill (1975, pp. 24–35) for a fuller discussion of the widespread folk-linguistic tendency to judge speech in terms of speakers. See also Halliday *et al.* (1964, pp. 98–107), Burling (1970, pp. 122–4), Giles (1970) and Trudgill and Giles (1976).
4. The present author regards IQ tests as pseudo-scientific. However, as Gahagan and Gahagan use such tests and also treat the scores as meaningful, these quotations are legitimate in terms of the Gahagans' frame of reference.
5. 'Bereiter and Engelmann . . . add an interesting note to their discussion when they observe that the listener may sometimes be deceived into believing that he hears some of the omitted items, whether sounds or words. The linguist would say that the reason the listener is led to believe this is that in fact he has heard something, even if it is not the same thing that he would have said in the context. Rarely are items simply left out of Child Black English or other variants of language.' (Houston 1971, p. 243)
6. See also the passage from Jensen (1968) quoted above.
7. In using the term *folk-linguistics* the present author is, of course, aware that the distinction between *linguistics* and *folk-linguistics* is by no means as straightforward as some linguists believe. However, the persistent use of value-judgements and other normative criteria place the verbal deficit theory unambiguously in the realm of folk-linguistics.
8. See Dale (1976, pp. 236–67) and Francis (1977, pp. 56–77) for a discussion of some of the main issues involved.
9. It is surprising that Classical Greek has not been the object of the most extravagant claims of all in this respect.
10. See Dale (1976, pp. 300–25) for a discussion of some of the difficulties involved in measuring language development and in relating test scores to actual speaking.
11. In this connection it is worth noting a report in *The Sunday Times* (6 August 1978, p. 13) by Carol Sarlar on tests used by ILEA to identify reading difficulties among schoolchildren aged about eleven. Sarlar writes:

Two of the three sections of the test ask children to fill gaps in a narrative. ILEA have forbidden us to quote the actual words, but parallels can be drawn — for example: 'He leapt up and _____ to the door in excitement. Adult graduates in this office put 'went' in that space, as did a majority of children in one London school last term. For that, the score was zero. Testers are told to accept only 'ran' or 'rushed.'

Presumably 'dashed' would also score zero. All this provides an excellent example of the arbitrariness necessarily entailed in psychometric and comparable forms of testing.

12. See Labov (1969).

13. Carroll (1956) gives a useful outline of the work and life of Whorf. Carroll (1964, pp. 106–11) discusses objections to the Whorfian hypothesis, and Dale (1976, pp. 237–41) discusses not only objections but also problems of interpretation.

14. Some linguists have attempted to formulate a non-deterministic variant of the Whorfian hypothesis, often referred to as the *weak version*. This latter version merely notes that certain categories and concepts can be more readily or conveniently expressed in some languages than others and suggests that this may have some influence on perception and categorisation.

15. For example, Whorf (1942, p. 247) states: 'Every language and every well-knit technical sublanguage incorporates certain points of view and certain patterned resistances to widely divergent points of view.'

3 BERNSTEIN'S SOCIOLINGUISTIC THEORY

In Britain by far the most important verbal deficit theory is that of
Basil Bernstein. It differs in a number of important respects from the
classical version of the theory, and at the same time presents a number
of difficult problems relating to scientific method and the presentation
of theories. Matters are further complicated by emphatic denials, made
by Bernstein from 1969 onwards, that he ever proposed a verbal deficit
theory. Most of the writers discussed in Chapter 2 were concerned, in
the first instance, with evolving, operating, describing and evaluating
compensatory language teaching programmes for children whom they
thought were handicapped by a verbal deficit, and for the most part
they are not primarily theorists. The theorising was largely secondary
to the practical teaching programmes and the research related to these.
In this respect Bernstein's position is very different, and his sociolinguistic writings contain no such programmes and offer virtually no
practical advice to the teacher. His research, and most of that of his
associates, is concerned primarily with exploring and vindicating his
ideas. Ultimately, his theoretical writings seek to provide an overarching
theory of socialisation and cultural transmission and, taken together,
they are conceived on a grandiose scale. Any examination of Bernstein's
theory immediately poses problems, some of them almost intractable.
The greatest difficulty of all is that he has not provided a comprehensive statement of his theory. By 'comprehensive statement' is meant
not, of course, an unalterable and final pronouncement but rather a
work of substance which deals with all the major aspects of a theory
and which summarises and largely supersedes earlier versions (where
such exist) and acknowledges and clarifies any ambiguities and contradictions that may have arisen in the course of the author's previous
writings. A comprehensive statement of this kind would have been
particularly valuable in the case of Bernstein's theory since his papers
display frequent changes in terminology, largely unacknowledged
shifts in focus, ambiguities and obscurities and, most confusing of all,
at least two outright contradictions. This last point calls for immediate
comment. First, the papers published between 1958 and 1965 propose
what, on any consistent reading, is a verbal deficit theory,[1] but
Bernstein (1969) strenuously seeks to deny this. Secondly, Jackson
(1974, pp. 65–6) notes that Bernstein (1965, p. 129) suggests that

codes control roles, while Bernstein (1971a, p. 177) suggests the very reverse! Such a major change would not necessarily have been confusing if it had been prominently acknowledged, but as Jackson (1974, pp. 65–6) observes:

> One is entitled . . . to ask what public notice has been taken, by Bernstein himself and by his colleagues and collaborators, of this reversal of position. The answer is, as far as I know, that no notice has been taken at all. The theory has continued to be respectfully quoted, as a continuously developing thing, without anybody noticing that it has in effect been retracted, and the opposite theory substituted. This is a phenomenon which may be unique in the history of science.

Part of the difficulty arises from the fact that Bernstein has put forward his theory, not in the form of a book, but in a series of papers. Although many of the most important of these have been published in a collection – *Class, Codes and Control, Volume 1* (= Bernstein 1971/74) – neither the introduction nor the postscript to that collection amounts to a comprehensive statement of his theory. Bernstein (1971b, p. 19) says himself that his papers 'are obscure, lack precision and probably abound with ambiguities'. Faced with problems such as these it is tempting to conclude that Bernstein hardly offers anything that can be regarded as a theory.[2] However, close scrutiny of his work reveals related and interlocking lines of thought which at least to that extent amount to a theory, though its consistency disintegrates rapidly from about 1969 onwards.

An elucidation is a prerequisite for any attempt to evaluate Bernstein's sociolinguistic theory. In view of the problems already outlined there are only two ways of examining the theory. Either one can examine Bernstein's work historically, tracing the various changes and developments, or one can try to cut through the inconsistencies and fluctuations in his work and attempt to provide an outline statement of the theory. The latter, if possible, would be highly desirable in view of Bernstein's failure to give any kind of comprehensive statement of his theory and the proliferation of unsatisfactory and inaccurate popularisations (by others) in some educational writings.[3] However, an outline must be preceded by a historical survey of his work, and for that reason both approaches will be used.

Bernstein's theoretical sociolinguistic writings can conveniently be divided into two periods: 1958–61 and 1962–73. Since 1973 he has published virtually nothing on sociolinguistics, though throughout the 1970s a considerable body of empirical work relating to his theory has been published by members of the University of London Institute of Education Sociological Research Unit, of which he is the head. But by about 1973 at the latest Bernstein's interests seem to have moved away from sociolinguistics, and in an Open University radio programme in 1973 he said that as far as he personally was concerned, the conceptual exploration of the theory of codes was completed[4] – a statement for which Jackson (1974, pp. 80–1) takes him severely to task. In his early work Bernstein postulates two dichotomous types of language having concomitant cognitive effects, and links between the social distribution of these types and that of differential educational attainment.

Bernstein (1958, pp. 24ff.) advances a theory of class-bound modes of perception and contends that the working classes and the middle classes are to all practical intents and purposes equipped with qualitatively different kinds of perceptual apparatus. This is stark expression of an extreme position. Though never repeated in these terms, this view that there are two fundamentally different types of perception, linked to social class, is implicit in much of his later work up to and including Bernstein (1971a) and is particularly prominent in Bernstein (1965, pp. 132–3 and 1970, pp. 143–8).

Although primarily concerned with social class and perception, Bernstein (1958) also outlines two qualitatively different, antithetical types of language which he associates with the class-bound modes of perception. He uses the term *public language* to denote the type of language associated with the working-class mode of perception and the term *formal language* to denote that associated with the middle-class mode of perception. Bernstein (1959) discusses the general regulative principles underlying public and formal language, but these two types of language are not identified with the regulative principles themselves; rather, they are seen as two general types of language each with its own distinctive characteristics. Bernstein conceives of public languages and formal languages, thus envisaging different varieties within each category. The purpose of referring in this chapter and subsequently to both categories as if they were unitary entities is to focus attention on the underlying dichotomy. This approach is legitimate in view of the fact that Bernstein offers very little discussion of the sub-varieties and also states that the terms refer 'to a common linguistic mode which various forms of communication, dialects, etc., share'.[5] The same principle is followed in the discussion of restricted code and elaborated code. On a linguistic level Bernstein's theory is ultimately concerned with what may, perhaps, best be described as two *macro-sociolects*.

Bernstein (1958 and 1959) provides a list of characterisations for both types. His main contention is that the lower (?) working classes can use only public language, while the 'middle class and associative levels'[6] can and do use both public and formal language. The characteristics of public and formal language are listed by Bernstein (1959, pp. 42–3 and 43n3) as follows:

Public language

(1)   Short, grammatically simple, often unfinished sentences, a poor syntactical construction with a verbal form stressing the active mood.

(2)   Simple and repetitive use of conjunctions (so, then, and, because).

(3)   Frequent use of short commands and questions.

(4)   Rigid and limited use of adjectives and adverbs.

(5)   Infrequent use of impersonal pronouns as subjects (one, it).

(6)   Statements formulated as implicit questions which set up a sympathetic circularity, e.g. 'Just fancy?' 'It's only natural, isn't it?' 'I wouldn't have believed it'.

(7)   A statement of fact is often used as both a reason and a conclusion, or more accurately, the reason and conclusion are confounded to produce a categoric statement, e.g. 'Do as I tell you' 'Hold on tight' 'You're not going out' 'Lay off that'

(8)   Individual selection from a group of idiomatic phrases will frequently be found.

(9)   Symbolism is of a low order of generality.

(10) The individual qualification is implicit in the sentence structure, therefore it is a language of implicit meaning. *It is believed that this fact determines the form of the language.*

Formal language

(1)   Accurate grammatical order and syntax regulate what is said.

(2)   Logical modifications and stress are mediated through a grammatically complex sentence construction, especially through the use of a range of conjunctions and relative clauses.

(3)   Frequent use of prepositions which indicate logical relation-
       ships as well as prepositions which indicate temporal and
       spatial contiguity.
(4)   Frequent use of impersonal pronouns (it, one).
(5)   A discriminative selection from a range of adjectives and
       adverbs.
(6)   Individual qualification is verbally mediated through the
       structure and relationships within and between sentences. That
       is, it is explicit.
(7)   Expressive symbolism conditioned by this linguistic form dis-
       tributes affectual support rather than logical meaning to what
       is said.
(8)   A language use which points to the possibilities inherent in a
       complex conceptual hierarchy for the organizing of experience.

Some may feel that it is unreasonable to quote a list that Bernstein
compiled over twenty years ago, especially as the theory has undergone
modifications since then. The reason for quoting these lists is that
they constitute the fullest set of superficially plausible recognition
criteria for his two dichotomous types of language presented anywhere
in his sociolinguistic writings.[7] Later writings contain definitions, and
recognition criteria have to be worked out on the basis of interpretations
of the definitions. In principle, of course, a general definition provides
a much more powerful instrument for identifying a sociolect than does
a mere list of characteristics. But even a formal definition is worthless
if one cannot derive from it linguistically sound and practically
applicable criteria for establishing whether an utterance is an example
of the one type of language or the other. The characterisation of
public language in terms of implicitness and of formal language as a
'language of explicit meaning' might conceivably form the basis for a
definition. However, Bernstein does not define his two types in these
terms in his published writings till 1969.
   At a casual glance the lists look like the kind of thing that might
enable a fieldworker (or anyone else) to identify an utterance as an
example of public or formal language. On closer inspection, however, it
soon becomes very clear that these lists offer virtually nothing that a
linguist can operate with, though the concept of sympathetic circularity
(characteristic 6, public language) has proved useful in sociolinguistics.
In both lists the first five characterisations contain a subjective
element, often compounded with value-judgements, and in both lists
the first characteristic relies on prescriptivist assumptions — that is,

notions of how language ought to be used, rather than observations of language as it is actually used. (Contrary to popular belief, descriptive, that is non-prescriptivist, concepts of language are not a recent, 'trendy' phenomenon, but have been generally taken for granted by most professional linguists for well over a century, though there have been some lapses. One of the clearest statements of this view of language is given by Sweet (1891, p. 1): 'The first business of grammar, as of every other science, is to observe the facts and phenomena with which it has to deal, and to classify and state them methodically.'[8]) Of the remaining eight characteristics, 9 and 10 (in the list for public language) and 6, 7 and 8 (in the list for formal language) are obscure. When Bernstein writes about 'individual qualification' he has in mind the way in which people express their reactions to events and circumstances.[9] Characteristics 10 (public language) and 6 and 7 (formal language) seem to relate to the kind of situation where one person reacts, for example to frustration, by saying 'Really! This is quite infuriating!' While another simply uses a 'four-letter word'. It is, of course, indisputable that the former structure is more flexible than the latter since there are a large number of adjectives that could be used in lieu of *infuriating*, and *quite* could be replaced by *highly* or *most*, etc. The total stock of 'four-letter words' cannot compete numerically with all these permutations. However, there is no good reason to suppose, as Bernstein does, that the one response 'blurs the nature of the experience' (Bernstein, 1959, p. 58) in a way that the other does not. Characteristic 7 (public language) is scarcely linguistic and 8 (public language) suggests the use of precoded chunks of speech.

Bernstein's contention that there exist two fundamentally different types of language, one superior to the other, and that the lower (?) working classes can use only the inferior type ought to have been presented either in a form allowing for empirical testing or as mere speculation. Despite the tentativeness of Bernstein's style (discussed by Coulthard, 1969, pp. 95–6) he certainly does not present his ideas to the public as untestable speculations. The experiments reported in Bernstein (1958 and 1960) and his later empirical work make it clear that Bernstein wanted to substantiate his ideas about the two types of language and their alleged cognitive effects. However, any real testing of his hypothesis is precluded by his failure to give adequate linguistic recognition criteria and also by his unsatisfactory handling of the concept of social class in these early papers.

Ideally, the concept of social class requires a definition of a class society and, within that context, of social class itself. This needs to be followed by a list of the classes in existence in a given society or type of society together with recognition criteria for each class and membership of it. If this procedure is followed it ought to be possible to assign any individual, or at the least any family or household, to one class or another on the basis of explicit empirical criteria. Such thoroughness is rare in British and American sociology, but all conventional categorisations of social class — whether stratificational, Marxist or pseudo-Marxist — have at least one feature in common: they all give reasonably clear criteria for assigning people to particular classes. Bernstein (1958, pp. 24—5) describes social class in terms that make this a practical impossibility. He begins by defining two social classes (working class and middle class and associative levels) in relatively familiar, stratificational terms. However, he has difficulty in establishing a clear distinction between the two. Ultimately he demarcates the two groups with uncompromising rigidity and does so in terms of family structures. If a well-developed theory of family typology and clearly established causal correlations between family structures and social class had been available in 1958 this approach might have yielded viable recognition criteria, but the necessary background was lacking then (as now). Even more interesting, however, is Bernstein's reason for dividing the population into social classes on the basis of family structure: one type of family, he claims, engenders one mode of perception, the other a quite different one. Thus to the extent that he defines social class in terms of family structure, he also does so in terms of the class-bound modes of perception which he himself has postulated. The reasoning in Bernstein (1958) amounts essentially to a circular series of propositions which can best be summarised as follows:

1. There are two distinct classes in society.

2. They are radically different because they perceive differently.

3. They perceive differently because their respective family structures are different.

4. The family structures in question are different and demarcate the two classes because these family structures induce different modes of perception.

5. The two classes perceive differently because one class (the working

class) lacks the type of language (formal language) that is a prerequisite for the mode of perception that characterises the other class (middle class and associative levels).

6. Differential educational attainment can largely be explained in terms of two dichotomous modes of perception, and the social distribution of educational attainment is accounted for by the class-bound nature of the two modes of perception.

Although Bernstein's next paper (1959) wavers on the question of linguistic determinism, the central tautology which gives rise to the circularity lies in the relationship between the third and fourth propositions, which he does not discuss again in any real detail in print till Bernstein (1970).

In order to convert these propositions into a testable theory it would, at the very least, have been necessary to define all the key elements involved – namely, social class, family structures, modes of perception and varieties of speech, perhaps even educational attainment – strictly independently of one another and in terms allowing for the derivation of appropriate and unambiguous recognition criteria. From there Bernstein might, in principle, have been able to proceed to formulate testable links between all the concepts which he sought to relate. This might have yielded an overarching theory open to empirical testing. But by introducing the concept of sociolinguistic codes in Bernstein (1962a) he committed himself to an even more ambitious variant of the pseudo-theory that he already had and at the same time removed it even further from the realms of scientific scrutiny. In effect what Bernstein had by 1960–1 was a set of interlocking propositions in which the main concepts and the links themselves were ill-defined or undefined. The hypothesis was that in some way all the concepts in his six propositions were related, but exactly how is something which he has never explained adequately.

The reason for giving a fairly detailed critique of these early papers is that the inadequacies in Bernstein's later sociolinguistic writings have their roots in his early work and in its fundamentally unscientific character. Taken together, his later writings on sociolinguistic theory amount to a kind of kaleidoscope. The chief ingredients – social class, family structures, modes of perception, dichotomous types of language and differential educational attainment – are all derived from his first two papers. (The main later additions are codes, roles and various kinds of meanings.) In each paper the kaleidoscope is reshuffled, usually without any acknowledgement of what is happening. On a fundamental level, the later versions of the theory fail to progress significantly beyond the muddle of 1958–9. Some may wish to object that Bernstein (1971b, p. 20) in effect admits that his sociolinguistic *oeuvre* does not amount to a theory: 'It is probably wrong to use the word "theory." The most we seem able to do is to construct weak interpretative frames.' It comes, therefore, as something of a surprise to find him saying something rather different a mere two years later in Bernstein (1973, p. 242): 'I have difficulty in understanding, and I have very little sympathy with, complaints that the socio-linguistic thesis of 1958 is in some respects different from the thesis in 1972.' However Bernstein may view his sociolinguistic writings, the fact of the matter is that what he actually presents in his published writings on sociolinguistics has the trappings but not the substance of a theory.

The terms *restricted code* and *elaborated code* are introduced in Bernstein (1962a). Public language and formal language were presented as types of language manifest in observable speech varieties: it was assumed that public language or formal language are actually spoken. This is not the case with a code, since codes are regulative principles governing speech: people do not speak restricted or elaborated code, just as they do not speak semantics, syntax or phonology.

Unlike grammar, which is a linguistic regulator, codes are at one and the same time linguistic, psychological and sociological in character. These three dimensions of the codes are discussed in most of Bernstein's papers and some give definitions of one or more dimensions. However, none of the papers presents a fully worked-out, integrated definition, and during the period 1962–73 there is a gradual shift in emphasis away from the linguistic to the sociological dimension. The best state-ment of the level on which the codes are postulated as having some kind of existence and of their extent is provided in Bernstein (1965, p. 131): 'The codes, linguistic translations of the meanings of the social structure, are nothing more than verbal planning activities at the psychological level and *only at this level can they be said to exist.*' (Bernstein's italics)

Bernstein defines the *linguistic* dimension of the codes in terms of relative syntactic predictability in Bernstein (1962a, pp. 76–7; 1964, p. 57; 1965, pp. 127–9; 1967, p. 22; and 1970, p. 145) and this definition is also foreshadowed in Bernstein (1961a, p. 291). In essence, he claims that in the case of speech regulated by elaborated code it is difficult to predict the syntax as the speaker will draw on a wide range of alternatives, whereas in the case of speech regulated by restricted code it is relatively easier to predict the syntax as the speaker will draw on a narrow range of alternatives and in extreme cases even lexis is predictable too. He claims that the lower working class — mysteriously quantified in Bernstein (1962a, p. 81), without reference to any source, as 29 per cent of the population — are limited to restricted code, while the rest of the population is able, at least potentially, to use language regulated by either code. The existence of the codes and their links with social class are taken for granted. What he is actually saying, for example in Bernstein (1962a), is that the speech of the lower working classes is highly predictable in terms of syntax, while with the rest of society this is not necessarily the case. As far as the linguistic dimension is concerned, the notion of codes is technically redundant.

The only relatively fool-proof way of testing these contentions about the relation between language and social class would be to make actual predictions and see if they were confirmed in the speech of large samples of people drawn from the working classes and the middle classes. It would also be necessary to match the contexts in which the speech was produced and to include a wide range of different contexts. This would be a major undertaking and, not surprisingly, Bernstein (1962a) tries to substantiate the point indirectly. He assumes that there is a correlation between syntactic predictability and the 'level' of verbal planning and, following Goldman-Eisler, that verbal planning correlates with hesitation phenomena. A high degree of predictability is associated with a 'low level' of verbal planning and this, in turn, is characterised by a relatively low level of hesitation and pausing. Conversely, a low degree of predictability is characterised by a relatively high level of hesitation and pausing. The actual conduct of the experiment carried out along these lines by Bernstein and reported by him in Bernstein (1962a) has been severely criticised by Coulthard (1969). The experiment merely tested hesitation phenomena and pausing — which were found to be more prominent among the middle-class than the working-class speakers. The notion that the former paused more frequently because they spent more time planning their utterances, and that therefore they planned their utterances in greater detail and their syntax was less predictable, is no more than a set of arbitrary assumptions. Apart from anything else, there is no way of establishing what people actually do when they pause and hesitate while speaking: they could, for example, just as well be thinking about *what* to say as *how* to say it. Moreover, people sometimes seem to use hesitation phenomena in conversation as a device for pre-empting interruptions. The most serious weakness of all, however, is that Bernstein (1962a) defines the linguistic dimension of the codes in terms of syntactic predictability and in the selfsame paper presents the results of an experiment which tests something else. As Lawton (1968, p. 94) points out, the codes are defined in terms of syntactic pre-dictability 'without . . . being tested by this criterion'. Finally, it should be noted that Hawkins conducted an analogous experiment sub-sequently and came up with very different results from Bernstein's. He divided his sample for both the working-class and middle-class subjects by sex, and found that by far the most fluent group of speakers was the working-class girls, followed by the middle-class girls, middle-class boys and working-class boys. In his report of the experiment, Hawkins (1973, p. 243) comments:

> Perhaps we need to question, then, our original assumption that greater fluency inevitably means less planning and hence inferior quality. It seems at least equally plausible to say that fluency indicates more experience, and/or greater confidence in language use on the part of the speaker and hence even *better* quality. Certainly, fluent speakers are often regarded as having greater control over their linguistic resources. Is it possible, then, that in the present case working-class girls are displaying greater, rather than less, linguistic expertise? (Hawkins's italics)

The definition in terms of syntactic predictability is used for the last time in Bernstein (1970), and a little later Bernstein (1971b, p. 8) virtually concedes that it is not viable. In other papers (1969, 1971a and 1973) Bernstein does not use this definition and, instead, retreats to implicitness and explicitness as the main linguistic characteristics of the two codes. These concepts are problematical. No speech is context-independent: everyone when speaking or writing makes assumptions about the listener, reader or audience. This is as true of instructions given to a complete stranger asking the way to the station as it is of the situation where a man simply calls 'Tea!' to his wife on returning home from work. The problem might appear to be one of quantification, but implicitness and explicitness are not quantifiable. It is possible to undertake comparative counts of exophoric, anaphoric and cataphoric pronouns,[10] or to compare one speaker's use of pronouns with another's more differentiated noun-phrase; but how, for example, would one set about measuring im-plicitness and explicitness in medical reports, law reports or in articles in learned periodicals, where the implicitness may reside in the lexis and in the author's assumptions about the reader's specialised knowledge rather than in any structurally identifiable features? Even the concept of exophoric versus anaphoric and cataphoric pronouns, as used by Bernstein (1969 and 1971a) and Hawkins (1969) and as disseminated by Lee (1973), is problematical, since it is interpreted in all these publications as strictly text-bound. If, on the other hand, one takes into account situational context, all the pronouns classed as exophoric in these writings (including the two now famous versions constructed by Hawkins of the story about the boys playing football) would fall into the anaphoric category.[11] All this adds up to a considerable weakening of the linguistic dimension of Bernstein's theory.

Before considering the other dimensions of the codes it should be noted that in Bernstein (1969) and subsequent writings there is increasing ambiguity as to the precise nature of the linguistic handicap of lower working-class children. Bernstein seems to be thinking now more in terms of a dichotomy in language-use (performance) rather than language in the strict sense (competence). This ambiguity is in fact present or at least latent in Bernstein's earlier papers, but it is only in and after 1969 that it becomes fully apparent. Bernstein (1971a, p. 173) accepts Chomsky's distinction between competence and performance and goes on to state (1971a, p. 179) that all children share the same basic linguistic rule-system, but that lower working-class children are uniquely restricted in the uses to which they can put this shared knowledge. In other words, they have the same language as other children, but cannot or simply do not use it to the same extent, or in the same way, or in the same kinds of situations, especially in the classroom. If this restriction were attributed to purely external factors, to 'sociological controls' as in Bernstein (1973a, p. 243) or 'contexts and conditions' as in Bernstein (1969, p. 197), this might be a tenable position. However, Bernstein (1971a, pp. 175–6) attributes the restriction primarily to differential access to elaborated code, and given the psychological nature of the codes the handicap must logically be a matter of competence as well as performance, unless the term *code* now means nothing more than an internalised 'code of behaviour'. As Jackson (1974, pp. 71–5) points out, by 1971 the term has in fact, to a considerable extent, taken on this sense. However, it has by no means entirely discarded its earlier senses, for Bernstein (1971a) still maintains that the codes act as psychological linguistic regulators, especially at the semantic level. In fact what has happened is that by 1971 at the latest the concept of

code as a linguistic regulator has become interwoven and confused with
that of code as a general behavioural regulator, at one and the same
time partly internalised and partly imposed externally. Since *all* human
activity, linguistic and non-linguistic, is subject to constraints of this
kind, the concept which Bernstein now has is not particularly useful
and the dichotomous model, to which he still holds, is virtually
meaningless. In view of the still essentially psychological nature of the
codes as linguistic regulators, the claim made by Bernstein (1973,
pp. 242–3) that he was 'At no time . . . concerned with differences
between social groups at the level of competency' must be rejected. It
is no exaggeration to say that Bernstein (1971a) marks the final
disintegration of the sociolinguistic theory.

The *psychological* dimension of the codes is the least developed in
Bernstein's work. Bernstein (1962a, p. 77) offers a brief definition,
and in Bernstein (1962b, 1964 and 1970) restricted code is seen,
psychologically, as a perceptual framework characterised by a strong
sense of group solidarity and the assumption that the attitudes and
feelings of others can largely be taken for granted. Conversely,
elaborated code is seen, psychologically, as a perceptual framework
characterised by a strong sense of individual identity and the assumption that the attitudes and feelings of others cannot be taken for
granted. This view is given some support by the findings reported in
Bernstein (1962b) on the use of egocentric and sociocentric sequences.
The fullest discussion of the codes in psychological terms is to be
found in Bernstein (1964 and 1970). In these papers the psychological
dimension of the codes is linked closely to implicitness and explicitness on the one hand and to social structure on the other.[12] But the
comparative neglect of the psychological dimension is strange, for
Bernstein assumes the following causal relationship between the three
dimensions:

sociological → psychological → linguistic

The psychological dimension is the mediator between the two
entities that Bernstein seeks to relate to one another – society and
language. But in Bernstein (1964 and 1970) – the two papers which
provide the fullest discussion of the psychological aspect – it is firmly
wedded to the sociological aspect. The psychological aspect is not
given the treatment which, as the mediating link between society and
language, it requires. Instead, Bernstein takes the link largely for
granted and offers generalisations like 'Restricted codes do not give
rise to verbally differentiated "I's" ' and 'The use of a restricted code
creates social solidarity at the cost of the verbal elaboration of

individual experience'.[13] Such statements do little to illuminate the psychological dimension and merely mystify the sociological and linguistic dimensions.

The social structure is seen as the ultimate generator of the codes.[14] The most detailed formulation of the *sociological* dimension is given in Bernstein (1970) where he tries to account for the psychological and linguistic dimensions in terms of social structures and, above all, family structures. The paper shows a shift in emphasis away from the linguistic dimension to the psychological and sociological dimensions. Bernstein is now much more interested in the content of what is communicated than in the characteristics of the linguistic means by which messages are conveyed. He claims that elaborated code tends to focus on the individual as an individual, while restricted code tends to concentrate on social roles. This difference is attributed to the different social environments in which the codes arise and the resulting dichotomy between solidarity and individualism. Ultimately, Bernstein links the notion of restricted code as 'a status or positional code' and of elaborated code as a code 'oriented to persons'[15] to his concept of *positional* and *person-oriented* family structures. He does this via the concepts of open and closed role systems and open and closed communication systems.[16] Open and closed role systems create open and closed communication systems and the latter in turn foster the development of restricted code and elaborated code respectively. He associates positional families with closed communication systems (and hence restricted code) and open communication systems with person-oriented families (and hence elaborated code). Bernstein's open and closed role systems and open and closed communication systems are in fact identical with the sociological and psychological dimensions of the codes. In a positional family the roles are based primarily on formal status, while in a person-oriented family the roles are to a much greater extent based on the attributes of the individual. Because the role system in person-oriented families is more fluid and less stable than in positional families, the individual members of the family have to rely heavily on verbal communication to achieve and maintain their roles. Similarly, the social control procedures used in the two types of family tend to be different: positional families rely largely on imperatives and appeals to the child's status, whereas person-oriented families rely to a much greater extent on appeals directed to the child as an individual. Thus the codes are often transmitted very early in life via social control procedures.

The reasoning in Bernstein (1970) is circular. The codes are defined here primarily in psychological and sociological terms and Bernstein then postulates two types of family structure which might reasonably be expected to foster the development of two different psychological perspectives corresponding to the two codes. Given Bernstein's initial assumptions about the character of the codes, and the terms in which the two types of family structure are postulated, his conclusion that positional families transmit restricted code and person-oriented families elaborated code is inevitable. Indeed, early in the paper he states that 'restricted codes could be considered status or positional codes whereas elaborated codes are oriented to persons'. The relationship between the codes and actual speech is now taken for granted, as is the relationship between the two types of family structure and social class.

If Bernstein's thesis on the relationship between family structure and code is correct, middle-class positional families ought on any consistent interpretation to orient their children to restricted code in the same way as working-class positional families, yet Bernstein seems to assume that all middle-class children acquire elaborated code. Despite the fact that the two types of family structure are initially advanced as structures which transmit one or the other code independently of class, the positional family is in fact equated with the lower working class, and the person-oriented family with all other social strata.

Various jargon-terms, such as *object* and *person modes* (of the codes), *universalistic* and *particularistic meanings* and *speech-models*, and the concept of roles, are added to the kaleidoscope at various points: they are not properly defined and are used in different senses in different papers. As noted above, even the meaning of the term *code* is unclear, confused and shifting. Commenting on this, Jackson (1974, p. 71) observes: 'Superficial woolliness in Bernstein is actually a rather clever device for masking a fundamental confusion of ideas.' Indeed, by 1971 the confusion had become so great that Josephine Klein (1972, p. 237), in a review of the first edition of Bernstein (1971/74), invoked the notion of genius to rescue him: 'It is difficult to discern from the introduction what Bernstein's own views are, but I personally hold that when a theorist of genius appears he can safely be left to evolve his own line of research.'

Without necessarily wishing to do so, Klein (1972) in effect appeals to a notion of 'genius's licence', akin to poetic licence, that supposedly frees Bernstein from normal scientific and academic constraints. The unstated analogy with poetic licence becomes very apparent towards the end of her review, when she suggests that the reader has to empathise with a particular state of mind in order to understand what Bernstein is saying:

> Perhaps properly to understand what Bernstein is after requires from the reader first of all an imaginative insight (spurious for all I know) into a state of mind which feels itself at once intellectually clumsy and sensitive to the point of paranoia.[17]

The view that Bernstein is so profound as to be comprehensible only to a handful of *cognoscenti* has been put to the present author by others. This kind of attitude says a great deal more about institutional sociology in this country than about those who refuse to enter into such a 'complicated state of mind' and who refuse to accept that 'the meaning doesn't matter . . .'.

Despite all the problems discussed it is possible to attempt to interpret Bernstein's ideas in 1970 and 1971, but of course it is not possible to offer anything more than an interpretation. In two papers (1970 and 1971a) Bernstein attempts to propose a series of causal relationships which seems to be as follows: social class → family structure → roles → modes of early socialisation → roles . . . modes of perception . . . access to codes → codes → speech → educational attainment. (An arrow indicates a link clearly postulated as such by Bernstein, dots an obscure link.) It should be noted at once that the entity 'roles' occurs twice and that the whole chain of causality is fuzzy from the second occurrence of 'roles' to 'access to codes' inclusive. Moreover both the first and the last links are simply taken for granted — namely, that between social class and family type and that between language and educational attainment. The general drift has become somewhat more complicated than in 1958 and 1959, but the theory has not progressed fundamentally. The usefulness of the middle categories is dubious in view of their obscurity and in view of the ambiguous lines of causality. However, ultimately the theory still represents an attempt to establish a causal relationship between social class, language (or language-use) and differential educational attainment. Shorn of inessentials, Bernstein's theory *might reasonably be taken to consist* of the following tenets:

1. The relationship between social class and differential educational attainment can largely be explained by postulating two dichotomous macro-sociolects which necessarily exist at the levels of both competence and performance. In the one (A), meaning is implicit; in the

other (B), meaning is explicit.

2. The lower working classes generally do not have access to, cannot
or simply do not use B (especially in situations where their teachers
expect them to do so), or can only use it to a limited extent and
subject to a wide range of psychological and other constraints, but the
rest of the population uses A and B quite freely.

3. B is a prerequisite for educational success, since this variety alone
holds the key to the 'universalistic', 'context-free' meanings which are
the real stuff of education. (A, by contrast, only provides access to
'particularistic', context-bound meanings.)

4. As lower working-class children generally lack B, or are severely
constrained in their use of it, they are for the most part doomed to
failure in the school-system.

5. The lower working-class children's lack of B, or unrestrained use of
it, stems primarily from the rigid ('positional') structure of the typical
lower working-class family.

  This statement of Bernstein's theory represents a deliberate and
obstinate attempt to make sense of the latter's writings and thus inevitably involves a considerable measure of subjective interpretation.
It is not a definitive statement of the theory. Indeed, the present
author stands by his previously expressed view that all that is possible
in the case of this theory is *interpretations*,[18] and of course interpretations other than that given above are possible. For example,
Jackson (1974, p. 68) writes:

  The central insight, I take it, was that one problem of education . . .
  is a conflict of value-systems between two classes, one valuing highly
  modes of thought and analysis which the other disvalued and tended
  to avoid; and that these value-systems are actually reflected in the
  language characteristically used, and perhaps transmitted by it.

Jackson has developed this interpretation in more detail:

  If an adult or an older child has a habit of expressing himself in a
  way that implies contempt for analytical concepts, he readily conveys information about his attitude to the younger child. Habitually

non-analytic modes of speech, implying a habitual hostility to analytical complexity, may thus be transmitted from generation to generation, without language-deficit of any kind being involved at any stage. I think this is what happens, in fact. It is a great puzzle to me that Bernstein did not all along prefer this version of the theory, which fits all the data much better, including that on child-rearing practices.[19]

One important point still remains. Is Bernstein's sociolinguistic theory a verbal deficit theory? The theory has obvious affinities with those discussed in Chapter 2. Bernstein seeks to account for differential educational attainment to a significant degree in terms of the alleged intrinsic attributes of two fundamentally different types of language. On the other hand, his theory is more sophisticated. He tries to look more closely at these alleged intrinsic attributes, linking them (often loosely and obscurely) with family structures, modes of perception and roles. Yet his theory still contains unexaminable and untestable psychological postulates (notably modes of perception and codes) and an ill-defined, socio-psychological concept (roles). Despite his attempts to offer a sociological theory, he relies heavily on psychological constructs similar to the 'x- and y-formulae' discussed in Chapter 2, and his restricted and elaborated codes are often used as global terms to cover these psychological aspects of his theory.

Further evidence that Bernstein's theory is one of verbal deficit is provided by the experiments reported in Bernstein (1958 and 1960). In the first experiment a test of verbal intelligence (the Mill Hill Vocabulary Scale Form I Senior) and a test of non-verbal intelligence (Raven's Progressive Matrices, 1938) were administered to 309 GPO messenger boys. As Bernstein predicts, the results show a significant overall discrepancy between the results on the two tests. Whereas the means for the verbal test all fall within the range 94—104 IQ, those for the non-verbal test cover a much wider range, namely 76—124 IQ. Thus for those subjects with very low or very high scores on the non-verbal test (the 71—80 and 121—6 IQ groups), the discrepancy between the mean verbal and the mean non-verbal IQ scores was found to be substantial (18—20 points). Bernstein (1958, p. 32) predicted that if the same tests were administered to a group of middle-class boys matched for age the relationship between verbal and non-verbal IQ scores would be found to be significantly different. Bernstein (1960) reports the results of an experiment designed to explore this difference. In this experiment Bernstein uses a fresh sample of working-class subjects, consisting of 61 messenger-boys, and a middle-class sample consisting of 45 public-school boys, both samples being matched for age. The tests used were the same as in the previous experiment. The results for the working-class sample are substantially in accord with those found in the earlier experiment, while those for the public-school sample show no comparable overall discrepancy between verbal and non-verbal IQ.

The results of these experiments are, of course, open to various interpretations. What is important, however, is Bernstein's own interpretation. In his discussion of both experiments he is particularly interested in the data showing a big discrepancy between high non-verbal IQ scores and near-average verbal IQ scores among working-class boys. Before conducting the first experiment Bernstein (1958, p. 30) predicted that: 'The higher the score on the matrices the greater the difference between the matrices and the Mill Hill scores.' And the experiment confirmed this prediction. The second experiment was preceded by the prediction (Bernstein 1960, p. 62) that: 'for the working-class group . . . the language scores would be severely depressed in relation to the scores in the higher ranges of a non-verbal measure of intelligence.'

Again, the experiment confirmed the prediction. Bernstein does not question the validity of the tests used; nor does he discuss the relationship between the verbal intelligence tested by the Mill Hill test and actual speech. In view of the fact that he treats the scores as meaningful, valid and reliable it would be hard to find a clearer statement of a theory of verbal deficit. Indeed, without a verbal deficit hypothesis, the predictions and the experiments would have been devoid of any rational motivation whatsoever. His true position in about 1960 is revealed very clearly in a comment made in Bernstein (1961b, p. 90) on the second experiment: 'The depressed scores on the verbal test for those working-class boys who have very high non-verbal scores could be expected in terms of the linguistic deprivation experienced in their social background.'

In Bernstein (1969 and 1973) the position is less clear. However, Bernstein (1971a, p. 176) states emphatically: *'One of the effects of the class system is to limit access to elaborated codes'* (Bernstein's italics).

Here Bernstein reverts to his dichotomous model of language, and claims that while one class has access to both, another (the lower working classes) has full access to only one and no more than partial access to the other. Given the link with education, this is a restatement of the verbal deficit hypothesis: the change from 'no access' to 'limited access' is of no real significance. There are also two highly revealing gaffes in Bernstein's later papers. Bernstein (1971a, p. 177) contains the now notorious imaginary conversation at the Millers — a eulogy on the (imaginary) speech of the intelligentsia. Bernstein (1969, p. 194 and 1971a, p. 178) also reproduce the now also famous two versions, constructed by Hawkins, of a story about children playing football. In fact, Hawkins (1969, p. 86) constructed these stories purely in order to illustrate differences between the use of pronouns and other, differentiated kinds of noun-phrase. Yet Bernstein quotes these versions as if they were typical of the speech of middle-class and lower working-class children respectively. Finally, it should be noted that many of Bernstein's papers contain a short, romantic section, usually no more than six lines long, on the aesthetic and metaphorical qualities of public language and, later, speech regulated by restricted code. This gesture to the qualities of lower working-class speech first appears in Bernstein (1959, p. 54):

> A *public* language contains its own aesthetic, a simplicity and directness of expression, emotionally virile, pithy and powerful and a metaphoric range of considerable force and appropriateness. Some examples taken from the schools of this country have a beauty which many writers might well envy. It is a language which symbolizes a tradition and a form of social relationship in which the individual is treated as an end, not as a means to a further end.
> (Bernstein's italics)

This passage is repeated almost verbatim in Bernstein (1961a, p. 308; 1965, p. 136; 1967, p. 34; 1971a, p. 186) and, in a much condensed form, in Bernstein (1970, p. 152). That Bernstein's early work proposed a deficit theory is beyond doubt, and his own denials cannot be accepted. As far as the later papers are concerned the issue hinges on the question of differential access to the codes. This point was summarised highly succinctly by a headmistress who was interviewed in connection with a research-project undertaken by the present author in 1977. When asked whether she regarded Bernstein's theory as a verbal deficit theory she replied:

> 'Yes, inasmuch as if there is a theory, he's saying, "These children have not, and the others have." . . . I was convinced that it was a deficit theory. It was only when he began to say it wasn't that I

began to wonder what it was.'[20]

Ultimately, any theory that seeks to explain differential educational attainment and its social distribution to any significant degree in terms of dichotomous types of language or language-use, with unequal social access to both, is a verbal deficit theory; and even by 1973 Bernstein had failed to break loose effectively and unambiguously from this kind of model.

Before concluding this chapter a few comments must be made on the large body of research associated with Bernstein's theory.[21] (Dittmar (1976) provides a valuable description and discussion of all the main research connected with both Bernstein's theory and the classical verbal deficit theory conducted and reported up to about 1971 and 1972, and Edwards (1979) provides useful outlines and evaluations of more recent research.)

Bernstein's theory is untestable. The most basic of all prerequisites for empirical testing is lacking – namely, a coherent statement of the general hypothesis. Moreover, his theoretical writings fail to provide clear definitions of the main concepts which he uses. As Dittmar (1976, p. 28) observes:

> In most cases the definitions are imprecise and metaphorical. The terminology is altered from one essay to another.
>   Bernstein's conception should be regarded as a hypothesis. As such, however, it has never been explicitly formulated.

In view of these problems, it is impossible to see how Bernstein's theory can be tested. A theory which is not stated clearly and coherently is not even a candidate for empirical testing. This raises questions about the relevance of experiments associated with Bernstein's theory. Although the research tests something, it is generally impossible to tell whether it tests the theory; yet often such work is cited as corroboration or support for the theory. In practice it has been all too easy to conduct investigations in the general area of language, social class, family structures and educational attainment and claim that the data support Bernstein's theories.

Notes

1.   For a discussion of Bernstein's theory as a verbal deficit theory, see pp. 83–6.

2.   Bernstein (1971b, p. 20) comments on his own work: 'It is probably wrong to use the word "theory." The most we seem to be able to do is construct weak interpretative frames.'

3.   Obviously, anyone wishing to give a brief outline of Bernstein's ideas in a more general book on education or the sociology of education is faced with a difficult task. In practice most popularisations by educationalists have been unsatisfactory and say nothing about the ambiguities or contradictions in the theory. Olive Banks, in the 2nd ed. of *The Sociology of Education* (1971, p. 93) states that 'public language is a language of nouns'. There is no justification for this statement in any of Bernstein's writings, and from a linguistic point of view there is no such thing as 'a language of nouns'. (In fairness to Banks, it should be added that this statement has been removed from the 3rd ed., published in 1976.)

Wilkinson (1971, p. 137) invites the reader to 'try to discern some of the characteristics of each code' from the following two passages:

(a) So me and Mike goes down to the museum / cause we had to didn't we / and we gets there / and we sees these dirty big statues all Greek and that / know what I mean / like at Euston there was a statue there in the caff /

(b) So Mike and I went down to the museum to see if we could get some ideas for our project / and when we got there we saw these large marble statues / I think it's considered they're mainly Roman copies of Greek originals /

To emphasise his point Wilkinson immediately adds: 'These useful distinctions between much "good" and "bad" English will probably receive considerable assent from the reader.' Thus Wilkinson establishes the following equations: (i) restricted code = non-standard dialect = 'bad' English; (ii) elaborated code = standard dialect = 'good' English.

Some educationalists have treated Bernstein's theory as if it were a matter of established fact. For example, Hornsey (1972, p. 34) writes:

The foreign language teacher must be able to rely on certain qualities in the learner. For example, the latter needs to be willing to make new sounds which differ from the accepted vocalisations of his everyday world; he has to have some notion that Western European languages make changes according to the time when events take, took or will take place; he has to be able to accept, for example, the existence of pronouns which are both personal and indefinite (French *on*, German *man*). Many children can do these things, but even a cursory glance at Bernstein's work will remind us that these needs will be real barriers for children who do not habitually use a public [sic] language, who will stubbornly refuse to speak with other than their local accent and for whom the rejection of this is yet another cause of conflict with the tone of school, who are not in the habit of using future tenses and who do not employ 'one' or its equivalents as indefinite pronouns. It is a nice question, but can we expect to teach 'elaborate' French to children whose use of their own language is 'restricted'?

4.   See Lee and Bernstein (*tape*, 1977).

5.   Bernstein (1959, p. 43).

6.   This is Bernstein's own term (see Bernstein, 1958). In general, there is considerable ambiguity in Bernstein's writings as to exactly which strata are, according to his theory, limited to public language or speech regulated by restricted code. He usually refers to the 'working class', but sometimes the 'lower

working class', 'the unskilled and semi-skilled strata' and at least once (Bernstein, 1970, p. 161) to 'the traditional working-class family'. Bernstein (1962a, p. 81) quantifies the strata in question (without reference to any source) as 29 per cent of the population. This figure suggests that at least at that time he had in mind the entire unskilled and semi-skilled strata.

7.   Bernstein (1962b, pp. 115–16) presents somewhat comparable lists derived from empirical data. However, the lists quoted above are the closest thing that he offers anywhere to actual recognition criteria.

8.   The descriptive principle was also adopted early in this century in some school text-books for English. One of the best examples is Rahtz's *Higher English*, first published in 1907. In the 4th ed. Rahtz (1909, p. 10) writes:

> Grammar consists of a logical statement and explanation of the rules and principles which govern our language at the present time.
>
> If we were to invent a new language we should probably begin with the creation of certain fundamental and important words. But before we had proceeded far, it would be necessary to formulate certain rules . . .
>
> It would be our aim to make these rules as simple and as of general application as possible; and we should take care as we proceeded further in the development of the language that all words and constructions strictly conformed thereto.
>
> But in the case of a language already in existence like English, Grammar comes not before the language, but *after* it . . . We have to take the language *as we find it* . . . (Rahtz's emphasis)

As always in such cases there is considerable room for debate as to how far the author succeeds in adhering consistently to the descriptive principle.

9.   See Bernstein (1959, p. 46n14).

10.   These terms, as now used in linguistics, have no direct connection with earlier senses in which they have occasionally been used in rhetoric. Instead, they relate to reference and, in particular, pronominal reference. An anaphoric pronoun refers back to a referent in the text, a cataphoric pronoun refers forward, and an exophoric pronoun refers to a referent outside the text. (Sometimes the anaphoric and cataphoric categories are grouped together as endophoric.)

Examples
(1) When Mary had finished supper *she* left the flat.   (anaphoric)
(2) *He*'s very good at maths, is John.   (cataphoric)
(3) *They*'re putting up the price of gas again.   (exophoric)

Although superficially simple, especially when applied to written texts, this classification is difficult to maintain if the context and not merely the text are taken into account, as is essential in any analysis of speech. In fact, genuinely exophoric pronouns are relatively rare (see Lodge, 1977).

11.   See Lodge (1977) and also a reply by Wales (1978).

12.   See especially Bernstein (1970, pp. 143–8).

13.   Bernstein (1970, p. 147).

14.   See Bernstein (1962a, p. 77; 1962b, p. 108; and 1965, p. 132).

15.   Bernstein (1970, p. 147).

16.   The terms *open* and *closed role systems* and *open* and *closed communication systems* are introduced in Bernstein (1970). These concepts are not developed in any detail either in that paper or subsequently and, as indicated, the open systems are no more than facets of elaborated code, while the closed

systems are corresponding facets of restricted code.

17. Klein (1972, p. 237).

18. See also Gordon (1978b, pp. 4 and 112–14).

19. From a personal communication (Dr L.A. Jackson to JCBG, 13 June 1979).

20. Gordon (1978b, p. 93).

21. See, for example, Oevermann (1972), Robinson and Rackstraw (1972), Cook-Gumperz (1973), Turner (1973), Adlam (1977) and Hawkins (1977).

4 CHALLENGES AND ALTERNATIVES

British linguists were slow to challenge Bernstein's theory. The first major attack came from Coulthard (1969), but it was not until about 1974 and afterwards that criticism began to appear on any large scale. In the USA, however, the response to the classical verbal deficit theory was much swifter, beginning in 1968. (In fact, much of the work on the classical verbal deficit theory and its main sociolinguistic rival, the 'difference theory', was carried out more or less concurrently.) In Britain and the USA opponents of the verbal deficit theory were largely concerned in each country with 'home-grown' versions of the theory. Thus in Britain the main target was Bernstein (and later Tough), whereas in America it was above all the classical version that came under attack. The work of the American opponents of the classical verbal deficit theory certainly had significant implications for Bernstein's theory, but the apparently widespread notion that Bernstein and Labov entered into a major direct confrontation is inaccurate, although they did attack one another's ideas very sporadically, in passing.

Since verbal deficit theories are by their very nature not amenable to empirical testing they cannot, of course, be disproved. This leaves two main avenues open to those who are sceptical of these theories. First, one can point out inadequacies, contradictions and obscurities in deficit theories and in the empirical work cited as supporting evidence. Secondly, one can offer alternative explanations for the questions that verbal deficit theories seek to answer. These two approaches are not mutually exclusive. The first mode of attack forms the basis of the critiques provided by Coulthard (1969), Rosen (1974), Jackson (1974) and Stubbs (1976a) and also plays a major role in Trudgill (1975), Dittmar (1976), and Edwards (1979).

The quest for alternative explanations to those offered by verbal deficit theories has taken a variety of forms. Among these have been restatements of the intelligence theory, for example by Jensen (1969), Eysenck (1971 and 1973), Herrnstein (1973) and Vernon (1978). Widespread disappointment with the short-term results of Project Head Start provided the immediate starting-point for these restatements of the intelligence theory in and after 1969, but other, more diffuse reasons played an important part in the renewed willingness to accept the theory. These probably included, in the case of the USA, defeat in Vietnam, and recurrent economic crises in nearly all Western countries after about 1966 which finally culminated in a world-wide slump after 1973. This general climate seems to have induced (especially in the USA) a spirit of widespread scepticism about the potential of education and its value to society. This scepticism found expression not only in a revival of the intelligence theory but also in the wave of 'deschooling' literature which began to appear at that time, and in Jencks *et al.* (1972). Tyler (1977), published in Britain, is also permeated with pessimism, despite attempts towards the end of the book to provide more optimistic guidelines for future educational policy.

There is still some room for debate as to whether all the Head Start programmes failed. The project, which was launched in 1965, sought to provide compensatory education and medical care for some socially and economically deprived sections of the population of the USA. The main object of the project was to ensure that as far as possible all children embarking on their statutory schooling would do so with certain basic minimum linguistic and cognitive skills. In educational terms this involved making available various forms of pre-schooling. These either provided formal training, or informal verbal and cognitive 'enrichment', or a combination of both. Head Start did not consist of a single blue-print, applied throughout the USA. By about 1970 it was widely held that Project Head Start had failed, though this early verdict has subsequently been challenged. Difficulties arise from the multiplicity of programmes used in Head Start and the problem of finding adequate criteria by which to assess their success or failure. In most cases, those monitoring the various programmes looked for an early increase in IQ scores (or scores on comparable 'objective' tests) sustained at the new, higher level during the first two or three years of statutory schooling. However, long-itudinal comparisons of the entire educational careers of a sample of children who had participated in a range of Head Start programmes with the educational careers of an appropriate control group would have provided a much better criterion. A recent report based on this kind of approach, Lazar and Darlington (1978), has come to relatively more favourable conclusions about a very small number of atypical programmes in Project Head Start.[1] It is not possible to give a definitive verdict on Head Start as a whole. Some of the programmes or sub-components may, for example, have been relatively successful in the longer term for reasons quite different from those originally envisaged (and therefore monitored) in the early stages of the project. This point was already raised by Little and Smith (1971, p. 53), who observed:

> The effects of Head Start on changes in . . . parental involvement, child health and so on are harder to assess; inevitably the comparatively clear-cut results from measures of educational performance are seen as the main indicators of success or failure. This is perhaps unfortunate at a time when the success of experimental preschool programmes in producing substantial gains is being re-examined as the evidence grows about the long term effects of such programmes.

Nevertheless, since 1970 very few have claimed that the specifically linguistic components of the various Head Start programmes were successful, either in themselves, or that they produced clearly identifiable cognitive 'gains'.

The psychometrists generally disregard several possible explanations for the failure of the linguistic and cognitive components of the programmes. One obvious explanation could be that the basis on which most of these components were conceived and carried out rested on the erroneous assumption that the children concerned were linguistically and cognitively deficient (in other words, the classical verbal deficit theory). This, combined with open contempt in many of the programmes for the children and the widespread reliance on dehumanising, behaviourist techniques of language-teaching, would provide ample explanation for the failure of any educational programme. The linguistic programmes used in Head Start were nearly all devised by psychologists who generally failed to recognise the interdisciplinary nature of the work they were doing and who seem to have made virtually no attempt to seek relevant comments and advice from linguists. The result was a plethora of folk-linguistic assumptions which happened to fit in with the social pathology model with which they were operating; and these assumptions accorded well with the more general outlook that lies at the very heart of much educational psychology itself, namely the view that failure to learn at school is in itself a sign of deficiency on the part of the child.

By far the most important alternative explanation to come to the fore during the late 1960s was what Dittmar has called the *linguistic variability hypothesis*, often referred to simply as the *difference hypothesis*. This hypothesis is based on a recognition of the well known fact — by no means new to linguistics — that the terms *English* and the *English language* (along with similar designations of other languages) refer to an idealisation. Since there are no purely linguistic criteria for distinguishing between a language and a dialect linguists normally have no alternative but to accept those distinctions that have already been established as the result of a combination of historical and political factors.[2] (The distinction has nothing to do with quantifiable linguistic differences.) In reality, a language consists of a collection of more or less closely related dialects which rarely, if ever, enjoy equal prestige among the speakers of the language. In the case of many languages, including English, one of the many dialects has in the course of time acquired such a measure of social prestige that it has come to enjoy the status of the 'standard' dialect, is used for all printed material and is the predominant dialect in all other public media of communication as well. Typically, this dialect is widely regarded as the language itself, and the idealisation is transformed into an imaginary monolith, as if English, for example, were or ought to be one and the same thing from Los Angeles via New York and London to Sydney and the Falkland Islands, and from the Shetlands via Edinburgh and London to Cape Town. The idealisation may serve to maintain a sense of linguistic unity among the speakers of the various dialects and may play some part in preserving a relatively high degree of mutual comprehensibility. It is also useful for many kinds of linguistic research.[3] Moreover, writing systems tend to foster this kind of idealisation. In most societies which have alphabetic writing systems and also enjoy widespread literacy the written version of the language tends to exercise a normative influence on speech and is generally regarded as in some sense superior. As Stubbs (1980, p. 30) notes: 'once a written language has developed in a community, it character- istically takes on something of a life of its own, and characteristically is regarded by its users as important and often superior as a form of language.'

Any writing system depends on a high degree of standardisation, and especially with the spread of schooling it tends to become in many respects increasingly rigid in its conventions. Partly because of its relative rigidity, and partly because writing is generally used for more prestigious purposes than speech, one often finds that the terms *English, German, French*, etc. are inaccurately equated with the written versions of these languages; and the obvious primacy of speech over writing is reversed in the minds of many people — even to the point where speech is regarded as a debased version of the written language. All this has the effect of further enhancing the status of the standard dialect.

The monolithic concept arises when the functional and conventional nature of the idealisation is ignored or blurred and the idealisation is actually equated with the language. Yet this monolithic concept itself is the culmination of the process which accords the standard dialect an increasing measure of prestige; for once a dialect is accorded standard status its further growth in prestige tends to become inevitable and self-perpetuating. This is a consequence of the historical process which originally conferred standard status on one dialect rather than another. In other words, the process does not stop when the standard dialect has become established as such. If a dialect is adopted by the ruling class, then those aspiring to ruling-class status and others who for whatever reason identify themselves with the ruling class will tend to adopt it, and it becomes the norm for all media of public communication. (In countries where the ruling class speaks a foreign language it is generally the intelligentsia that establishes the standard.)

The role of the various media of public communication in enhancing the prestige of the standard dialect is very considerable. Access to these media is severely limited and few people can ever expect to play an active role in them. Most people are placed in the role of mere recipients. Despite the introduction of 'phone-in' radio programmes, the ordinary citizen's chances of making his views known to the public by means of the established media hardly extend beyond a reader's letter in a local newspaper. In practice, a situation arises where those who participate actively in the public media of communication either already enjoy a measure of esteem or prestige before playing any active part in them, or tend to be credited with these attributes soon after they begin to participate. One finds a subtle interplay between the prestige of the media themselves, of those who participate actively in them and of the preferred linguistic varieties used in the media.

An inevitable concomitant of monolithic views of language is a wholesale disvaluation of all dialects other than the standard. Non-standard dialects come to be regarded as substandard or are even denied the status of language altogether, as was apparent from some passages cited in Chapter 2. One nearly always find a hierarchy among the non-standard dialects, with those generally spoken by the Negro population at the very bottom of the scale in the USA and England. The whole hierarchy, including the ambivalent status accorded to rural dialects in England and Germany, is a reflection of widespread social attitudes. Recognition of the social disvaluation of non-standard dialects forms the basis of the linguistic variability hypothesis. Dittmar (1976, p. 104) summarises the main tenets of the variability hypothesis and the main guiding principles of its proponents:

1. Any meaning which is relevant to . . . understanding between people can be expressed in any language.
2. In accordance with (1), *socially-determined speech differences are of a non-cognitive type unless there is empirical proof to the contrary*. The non-cognitive analysis of speech differences is based on the idea that for each linguistic utterance in A there is a corresponding utterance in B (A and B can represent styles, standards, dialects or functional varieties), which conveys the same semantic information (synonymy). Differences between A and B in respect of certain linguistic features are only understandable on the basis of a comprehensive contrastive analysis of A and B on all levels of grammar.
3. In the sense of (2), the description of speech variation is concerned with the type and degree of structural and functional interference, as well as the social relation and interaction between two given linguistic systems. (Italics – JCBG)

The italicised statement represents the central proposition of the linguistic variability hypothesis. Since it actually mentions proof (and thus by implication also disproof) it may at first sight present the appearance of a testable hypothesis. However, the variables – *speech differences, socially-determined, of a non-cognitive type* – are so vague and elastic that it is impossible to envisage valid tests. The statement amounts in effect to a simple denial of a 'strong' version of the Whorfian hypothesis. This becomes particularly clear if one also considers Dittmar's statements about synonymy. Here, too, it is impossible to envisage valid tests. Even if one considers other formulations of the hypothesis the possibility of empirical testing is, to say the least, extremely remote and it may ultimately be necessary to conclude that the linguistic variability hypothesis is not strictly testable. This would not, of course, mean that all the assumptions underlying it were unjustified, still less that the work of its adherents was worthless. Among linguists, there appear to be some who fear that a rejection of the claims of the linguistic variability hypothesis to scientific status would leave the way open for value-judgements on relative intrinsic 'merits' of different dialects and languages. This fear is unnecessary. First, all languages and dialects are immensely complex. Secondly, in those cases where it has been claimed that a particular language or dialect is primitive, substandard or deficitary, linguists have so far found it fairly easy to discredit such claims as based on inadequate observation, unsatisfactory analysis or extraneous factors, such as racial or class prejudice. Thirdly, there is no meaningful way of measuring the relative complexity of different dialects or languages, either quantitatively or otherwise.

The linguistic variability hypothesis was not evolved in an ideological vacuum. It was conceived in direct opposition to the classical verbal deficit theory and those components of Head Start which were based on the deficit theory. Not surprisingly, it bears the marks of this confrontation. Although Dittmar's formulation of the linguistic variability hypothesis is expressed in very general terms, the adherents of the hypothesis were very largely concerned with the standard dialect of English and Black English Vernacular (BEV). In order to counter the claims of the classical verbal deficit theory they sought to demonstrate that the American Negro dialects are as regular as the standard and differ from it in a systematic manner, that those who speak these dialects are as capable as others of abstract and sophisticated thinking, and that these dialects do not contain any mysterious blight that might impair cognitive development or educability. Works such as Labov *et al.* (1968), Labov (1969), Baratz (1969 and 1970a), Baratz and Baratz (1970), Cazden (1970) and Houston (1969 and 1971) were conceived, in somewhat varying degrees, in this spirit and with these ends in view. The ultimate goal, especially in the case of Labov's work, was to demonstrate decisively that BEV is equal, indeed largely equivalent, to the standard dialect, but merely differs from the latter in respect of a number of grammatical and other rules which can be accommodated (by means of variable rules) within the framework of a transformational-generative grammar of the standard dialect. From the point of view of linguistics the chief weakness of this approach lies in the notion of 'as . . . as . . . '. This presupposes that it is possible to measure the relative complexities of different dialects in some meaningful way, for example by means of some kind of quantification. However, such quantifications are meaningless in comparisons between dialects and languages. First, there is no agreed or reliable yardstick on which calculations of this kind could be based, so the actual results would depend on the yardstick selected. Secondly, even if a reliable and agreed yardstick could be found — which is highly doubtful — it is impossible to see what meaningful interpretation could be placed on a finding that one dialect has x rules, whereas another has $x - y$ rules. Such a finding would be no more than a curiosity.

In the long run, renewed endeavours to investigate the history of the Negro dialects spoken in the USA, Jamaica and elsewhere provided a more fruitful basis for the study of these dialects as linguistic systems in their own right, with a history of their own quite different from that of other English dialects.[4] Work in this field had hitherto been relegated to the periphery of linguistics. Important new studies included Bailey (1965), Cassidy (1968), Dillard (1968 and 1972), Stewart (1970) and Traugott (1976).

Despite the theoretical weaknesses of the linguistic variability hypothesis, its adherents *did* succeed in discrediting the work undertaken by the proponents of the classical verbal deficit theory and in making the theory itself look highly implausible. (As already noted, the theory is not open to empirical testing and therefore cannot be disproved.) The vigorous attack by Labov (1969, p. 34) on the classical verbal deficit theory is still valid:

> There is no reason to believe that any nonstandard vernacular is in itself an obstacle to learning. The chief problem is ignorance of language on the part of all concerned. Our job as linguists is to remedy this ignorance: Bereiter and Engelmann want to reinforce it and justify it. Teachers are now being told to ignore the language of Negro children as unworthy of attention and useless for learning. They are being taught to hear every natural utterance of the child as evidence of his mental inferiority. As linguists we are unanimous in condemning this view as bad observation, bad theory, and bad practice.
>
> That educational psychology should be so strongly influenced by a theory so false to the facts of language is unfortunate; but that children should be the victims of this ignorance is intolerable.

From the point of view of linguistics, this is perfectly sound. It also suggests a partial explanation for the social distribution of educational attainment: certain groups of children are viewed as predetermined to failure, as ineducable, and even regarded with contempt by large numbers of teachers, and this mentality is encouraged by at least certain schools of thought in educational psychology. (It might be added that psychometry fostered very similar views on the part of teachers with regard to the same sections of the school population.) However, as Michael Stubbs has observed, 'You have to choose your educational policy separately from your linguistic theory.'[5] As far as educational policy is concerned the only points that arise in any obvious way from the linguistic variability hypothesis may be summarised in the form of four axioms for teachers and those responsible for teacher-training:

1. Teachers must *understand* the dialect(s) spoken by their pupils.

2. Teachers must be as fully aware as possible of those features of their pupils' dialect(s) that differ from the standard and are therefore likely to be misinterpreted as mistakes.

3. Since all dialects are intrinsically equal from a linguistic point of view it is pointless to try to make pupils *speak* the standard dialect. (Any pupil who wishes to acquire the standard dialect can do so easily enough, as there is nowadays no lack of models available to pupils. Teachers should not think that they provide the only opportunity for this, and there is no place for any attitude among teachers that they have some duty to preserve the 'purity' of the language.)

4. Due allowance must be made for the fact that the mismatches between speech and writing will vary according to the pupil's dialect and accent. In particular, teachers must not assume that there is a standard mismatch for all pupils corresponding to the difficulties in reading and writing typically encountered by pupils who speak the standard dialect with a more or less standard pronunciation.

Beyond these four axioms, however, the variability hypothesis does not in itself offer any obvious guidelines for educational policy, and the axioms leave vast areas of great importance untouched. For example, should pupils be taught to write exclusively in the standard dialect? As for the question of the distribution of differential attainment, the variability hypothesis itself cannot offer any explanation other than ignorance, intolerance and prejudice on the part of teachers, which presumably have the effect of alienating the child from the school. In order to go further than this in accounting for the distribution of educational attainment and in the formulation of educational policy it is necessary to add to the linguistic variability hypothesis. Labov *et al.* (1968), Labov (1969) and others, including for example Baratz and Baratz (1970), noted extensive, distinctive cultural (or sub-cultural) features among the populations of the Negro and Puerto Rican urban ghettoes. These writers adopted the widely accepted sociological distinction between 'mainstream' and 'non-mainstream' culture and in some cases, for example Labov (1969) and Baratz (1970b), write as if communities speaking a non-standard dialect automatically have a non-mainstream culture. Part of the reason for this ready acceptance of a parallel cultural dichotomy may be attributed to difficulties encountered in demarcating dialects. What is at issue for the proponents of the variability hypothesis, as far as educational policy is concerned, is not so much dialects as such but rather *groups* of non-standard dialect-speakers forming an identifiable speech-community, and it is usually impossible in America (or Britain) to identify such communities without having recourse to cultural as well as linguistic criteria. Hymes (1970, p. 73) comments:

> First of all, what counts as a language boundary cannot be defined by any purely linguistic measure. Attitudes and social meanings enter in as well. Any enduring social relationship or group may come to define itself by selection and/or creation of linguistic features, and a difference of accent may be as important at one boundary as a difference of grammar at another . . .
> Secondly, speech communities cannot be defined in terms of linguistic features alone in another respect. Their definition must comprise shared knowledge both of one or more of the primary varieties, and of rules for their use. Differential knowledge of a linguistic variety aside (and that is of course of importance), a person who is a member of a speech community knows not only a language but also what to say.

Most proponents of the linguistic variability hypothesis urge the need for due recognition of non-mainstream culture among non-standard speech-communities. This concept is used both as a partial explanation for educational failure and as the basis for educational policy designed to open a path into the mainstream culture for children in such communities. In general terms, these aspects of the variability hypothesis have been summarised succinctly by Williams (1970, p. 5):

> Like the proponents of the deficit position, the difference theorists agree that the poverty child is failing in our schools and that something has to be done. But where the former would focus much of the remediation upon the child's apparent unreadiness for school, the difference theorists tend to accuse the school of unreadiness . . . They are arguing that the United States is a poly-cultural society with monocultural schools, and that this is the first

and perhaps most damaging inequity foisted upon the poverty child.

But the ultimate policy goal of the proponents of both theories is
similar — acculturation of the minority to the mainstream. This
becomes clear if one looks at the actual policies proposed by most
of the American advocates of the variability hypothesis. Their long-
term educational objectives are in fact conventional. Labov (1972)
and Baratz (1970b) are concerned to find ways of ultimately making a
relatively conventional ('mainstream') education genuinely available to
economically and socially deprived children. Their proposals are un-
conventional only to the extent that they insist that for children in
communities with non-mainstream cultures it is first necessary to build
a bridge between the two cultures and that such children (and their
teachers) must be equipped with the necessary linguistic and cultural
training to enable the pupils to profit from a conventional education.
Although there are differences in emphasis between Labov and Baratz,
neither sees the systematic incorporation into the curriculum of
elements drawn from the local culture as anything other than instru-
mental in achieving this goal. For example, Labov (1972, p. 5) proposes
the following list of priorities for pupils in ghetto schools:

a. Ability to understand spoken English (of the teacher).
b. Ability to read and comprehend.
c. Ability to communicate (to the teacher) in spoken English.
d. Ability to communicate in writing.
e. Ability to write in standard English grammar.
f. Ability to spell correctly.
g. Ability to use standard English grammar in speaking.
h. Ability to speak with a prestige pattern of pronunciation (and
   avoid stigmatized forms).

The chief difference between this kind of approach and that derived
from the classical verbal deficit theory appears to lie in the strategy
proposed, as well as a much more sympathetic attitude towards non-
standard dialects. The strategy proposed here and also in most contributions to Baratz and Shuy (eds., 1969) and Fasold and Shuy
(eds., 1970) is essentially that of bi-dialectalism. The teacher accepts
the child's dialect, initially concentrates on fostering and encouraging
linguistic communication *per se*, making full use of the local culture,
and subsequently proceeds to initiate the child in the conventions of
the standard dialect. For Labov (1972) this process includes teaching a

standard pronunciation. Here Labov's proposals actually run counter to one of the axioms deduced from the variability hypothesis, and in general his priorities differ, at least in emphasis, in several respects from the four axioms listed earlier. The justification offered by Labov (1972, p. 7) for teaching the standard dialect and a standard pronunciation is severely practical: unless they speak in this way, Negroes will be stereotyped and discriminated against. Many subsequent studies, for example Williams (1973), Shuy and Williams (1973) and Taylor, O.L. (1973) in the USA, and Giles and Powesland (1975), Trudgill and Giles (1976) and Macaulay (1977, pp. 91–130) in Britain, have demonstrated the complexity, extent and depth of prejudices against non-standard dialects and accents. Yet there is an underlying contradiction in Labov's strategy, for in the last analysis it is groups of the population, social classes, that are stigmatised, and the status generally accorded to their dialects and accents is no more than a reflection of this. It is of course true that speech is often one of the most important and immediately obvious badges of social class membership. Rosen (1974, pp. 1–2), discussing verbal deficit theories, writes:

> As the scholarly scrutiny of the life-habits of the working class proceeds, more and more attention has focused upon their language (which as everyone knows distinguishes them from others much more effectively than, say, horny hands and overalls).

Even if Labov's policy of full bi-dialectalism were successful and schools turned out Negro and other working-class children speaking the standard dialect with the appropriate standard pronunciation, it would be extremely naive to assume that they would automatically be distributed across the occupational spectrum in the same kind of proportions as the general population. At best, bi-dialectalism might go some small way towards facilitating upward social mobility, a point acknowledged by Baratz (1970b, p. 26n6) when she writes:

> I do not wish to suggest that the use of standard English by black children will insure their success in middle class white America or that it will erase prejudice against Negroes, nevertheless, since standard English is the language of the mainstream it seems clear that knowledge of the mainstream system increases the likelihood of success in the mainstream culture. (Original punctuation retained)

It is, in fact, very difficult to find any convincing *rationale* for a policy of bi-dialectalism. The claim that bi-dialectalism is a prerequisite for literacy is unsound. As far as reading is concerned, the main point at issue is that teachers must not equate ability to read with ability to read out loud in the standard dialect or with any particular 'standard' pronunciation. They must make allowance for the fact that there is no single mismatch between speech and writing.[6] With writing, the question is partly one of what society (and, in particular, teachers) will tolerate, and partly one of conventions regarding spelling and style; but the notion that children cannot learn to write standard English unless they speak it is untenable. Ability to read, together with explicit instruction in the conventions of written English, provide a sufficient basis for learning to write. This points to a policy of reorientating teacher-training rather than to a policy of bi-dialectalism. But even where teachers are relatively intolerant of non-standard dialects children generally seem to be fairly successful in learning to read and write. However, perhaps the most telling argument against the notion that ability to speak the standard dialect is a prerequisite for literacy is the fact that some people are able to read and even write a foreign language even though scarcely able to speak it. The case for teaching children to speak the standard dialect is thoroughly obscure. In a society where children have ready access to material printed in the standard dialect, to radio and television, individuals have in any case the opportunity to acquire the standard dialect and also a prestigious pronunciation if they so wish. Indeed, many children make use of these opportunities and either become bi-dialectal or discard their native dialect altogether in favour of the standard dialect or a close approximation to it. Thus any policy of bi-dialectalism would be aimed specifically at children who, for whatever reason, have in some sense chosen not to speak the standard dialect. In these circumstances a policy of bi-dialectalism would encounter resistance and would lend itself to interpretation as a systematic attempt on the part of the schools to eradicate non-standard dialects.

As far as educational policy is concerned, the proposals advanced by the British sociolinguist, Trudgill, are more fruitful. Trudgill (1975, pp. 46–85 and 102–3) carefully considers the question of accent, dialect and educational policy and comes to very different conclusions from those of the majority of American proponents of the variability hypothesis. He argues in favour of a policy of tolerating and even encouraging diversity in accents and dialects in school and, more generally, fostering a much more tolerant attitude towards linguistic diversity in society as a whole. Apart from mere tolerance and encouragement, this would involve the systematic demystification of the standard dialect and explicit discussion of attitudes towards dialects and accents. In short, he pleads for the elimination of ignorance and prejudice on these matters in much the same way as does Labov (1969). But in direct contrast to Labov (1972), Trudgill (1975, p. 65) notes: 'We have seen that dialect differences in British schools do not constitute an education problem *unless* standard English is required of children who have some non-standard variety as their native dialect' (Trudgill's italics).

This is in keeping with the four axioms and Trudgill's principle of linguistic toleration. It is also intuitively sound, for few endeavours seem to meet with less success in school than attempts to make unwilling pupils speak the standard dialect or to alter their pronuncation. Moreover, it is important to be aware of the sheer magnitude of the task that such attempts involve. Trudgill has estimated that of the adult population of England (excluding Wales, Scotland and Northern Ireland) only 15 per cent speak the standard dialect and of these, only about one-seventh or approximately 2 per cent of the population use RP (Received Pronunciation).[7] On the other hand, any attempt to create widespread and genuine tolerance of linguistic diversity in society in general would also be an extremely difficult and slow undertaking. Interestingly, two American adherents of the variability hypothesis, Fasold and Shuy (1970, pp. ix–xvi), consider this approach as an alternative to bi-dialectalism but are sceptical on practical grounds. Moreover, in Britain there was a radical shift in official attitudes on this issue between 1937 and 1954. Before the Second World War the Board of Education favoured a policy of bi-dialectalism, but in 1954 the Ministry of Education strongly urged the cultivation of tolerance towards linguistic diversity. (This change is discussed in Chapter 5.)

There is of course a certain paradox in Trudgill's proposals for the toleration of linguistic diversity. Since attitudes to varieties of speech derive from attitudes towards groups of speakers, and since the latter are in turn related to social status, it might be argued that nothing can be achieved without fundamental changes in the structure of society itself. Although there is some substance in this view, current attitudes towards linguistic diversity are often harmful. For example, individuals are frequently judged on the basis of their speech. This is well known, and has been demonstrated for example by Giles (1971). In an experiment using the matched-guise technique he found that general judgements, often concerning important attributes of the individual, were based on accent. Giles (1971, pp. 714–15) reports as follows:

A two minute tape-recorded prose passage was read in three accents (RP, mild south Welsh and Somerset) by two male speakers, and this was played to listeners who were asked to evaluate the voices on 18 adjective traits (for example, generous-mean, intelligent-dull). The notion of 'accent' was never introduced and listeners were told that their immediate impressions from the voice was all that was wanted. Besides certain interesting age, regional and personality differences, a distinct pattern of values emerged. We found that RP speakers were seen more favourably in terms of their competence (their ambition, intelligence, self-confidence, determination and industriousness) but less favourably in terms of personal integrity and social attractiveness (their seriousness, talkativeness, good-naturedness and sense of humour) than the regional speakers.

Unfortunately, Giles says very little about the social background of the listeners in this particular experiment, which might have put the latter part of these findings into a clearer perspective. However, most readers will no doubt be quite familiar with the kind of phenomena described in this passage, and there is also a wealth of anecdotal evidence which accords with many of his findings.

There is much that teachers can do to encourage tolerance of linguistic diversity. First, and most obviously, they must tolerate it themselves along the lines advocated by Trudgill (1975). Secondly, they are well placed to make the nature of linguistic prejudices, both towards dialects and speakers, utterly *explicit*. (There is no need to wait for major social changes before embarking on this.) By openly discussing the reasons why there is a hierarchy of prestige among dialects, and by exposing linguistic and other prejudices about speakers and the connotations and stereotypes on which such prejudices are based, they could go some way towards eradicating the kind of widespread ignorance that Labov (1969) deplores. This kind of discussion could, perhaps, be most usefully undertaken at the time when adolescents seem to begin to approach an adult level of linguistic awareness (probably from age 13+ onwards). With younger pupils, it ought to be possible to stress the essentially conventional nature of language, and to do so explicitly. For example, teachers might discuss conventions relating to differing levels of formality in style. Overall, this strategy would do something to demystify the standard dialect and the problems arising from this mystification. It would be a mistake, however, to regard Trudgill's suggestions as a solution to problems of social inequality. The fallacy of such a view is evident from the following passage written by an American adherent of the variability hypothesis, O'Neil (1968, p. 15):

> Instead of 'enriching' the lives of urban children by plugging them into a 'second' dialect . . . we should be working to eradicate the language prejudice, the language mythology, that people grew into holding and believing. For there is clear evidence that the privileged use their false beliefs about language to the disadvantage of the deprived. One way to stop this is to change non-standard speakers into standard dialect speakers at least for some of the time, i.e. when the non-standards are in the presence of the standards, currying favor of them, jobs from them, etc. This seems to me intolerable if not impossible. Another response to language differences would be to educate (especially the people in power) for tolerance of differences, for an understanding of differences.

Neither of these approaches will actually prevent those in positions of power from acting 'to the disadvantage of the deprived'. The real justification for Trudgill's proposals is rather different. First, tolerance of diversity would save valuable time often now wasted in schools on linguistic trivia and on compensatory language programmes. Secondly, it would enhance the self-respect of pupils with non-standard dialects and regional accents. Thirdly, a policy of linguistic tolerance and systematic demystification would expose one of the most widely used (and readily available) criteria for stereotyping people – a criterion which still often masquerades as using or not using 'good English'. Fourthly, in this respect such a policy would constitute a challenge to all who judge people by their speech. Finally, open discussion in schools of attitudes towards linguistic diversity could form a useful basis for the discussion of other, equally harmful stereotyped attitudes and even of the mechanisms of stereotyping in general. These points, together with the fact that there are no objective criteria for evaluating any dialect as intrinsically superior or inferior to any other, provide an adequate justification for Trudgill's plea for the toleration of linguistic diversity in schools and in society at large. Fortunately, the frequent appeals in Trudgill (1975) to the linguistic variability hypothesis are entirely redundant to his case.

Before leaving the linguistic variability hypothesis altogether, a few comments may usefully be made about a school of educational thinking that has largely fastened on the cultural, rather than the linguistic, aspect of the work of Labov and others. This school of thought, which was referred to very briefly towards the end of Chapter 1, tends to see traditional curricula as largely alien and meaningless to the cultural values of working-class communities, as the embodiment of mainstream culture or, to use the popular catch-phrase, 'the bourgeois values of the school'. Adherents of this view often argue that all curricula are of intrinsically equal worth and generally plead for the adoption, especially in working-class areas, of specifically community-based curricula: thus history, at middle-school and upper-school level, becomes local social history, English becomes the study of 'working-class literature', geography is based as far as possible on the immediate locality or region, while modern languages come to be seen as an irritating slot in the timetable to be filled with something that can be passed off as French, German or whatever language is officially supposed to be taught.[8] With mathematics and the natural sciences, this approach immediately runs into serious difficulties, though even here there is occasionally scope for concentrating on matters of particular local interest.

The motives underlying these philosophies of intensely local curricula are varied — sometimes, perhaps, an extreme reaction against the traditional grammar school curriculum; more often, perhaps, a rebellion against the extent to which education seems to elude effective democratic control. But whatever the motives and the rhetoric, two assumptions stand out clearly: first, that a common curriculum is impossible, and secondly, that anything closely resembling the mainstream, allegedly 'bourgeois' curriculum is particularly inappropriate for working-class pupils. What is overlooked is that *all* children in Britain and their parents live in one and the same nation-state, under one and the same political, economic and social order. Localising the curriculum can only have the effect of artificial segregation, and it is also very much open to question how many schools are actually located in identifiable communities with clearly defined cultures of their own.

It is significant that, when pressed to identify specifically bourgeois characteristics of the school, adherents of community-based education tend to point in the first instance to the invisible curriculum — in particular competitiveness, obedience to those in authority, stress on personal tidiness in physical appearance and dress (including school uniform). With the possible exception of competitiveness, it is difficult to make out a convincing case for regarding these values as specifically bourgeois. Where the visible curriculum is concerned, there is certainly a need for debate about clashes between differing subcultural values, especially in relation to the Classics, English and music, but hardly in connection with other subjects. With the latter, a much more fruitful area of discussion would surely be the question of *bias* rather than differences between 'high' and 'low' subcultural values.

In general, much of the discussion about conflicts between middle-class and working-class (and also mainstream and non-mainstream) cultures is based on very simplistic concepts of culture in a complex society. Vast areas of overlap where there is a common culture are often ignored, as are also the broadly unifying cultural influences of the media and the effects of more or less centralised political and economic control within a nation-state; while insufficient attention is given to the kind of cultural influences that schools actually do exert, to the values that they seek to impart and in fact succeed in transmitting. At its worst, the discussion degenerates into pseudo-radical rhetoric on the one hand and fastidious aestheticism and snobbery on the other. Chanan and Gilchrist (1974, pp. 31–70) try to unravel some of the complexities involved in the concept of culture in contemporary English society, with particular reference to the school. They stress that culture is made up of different strands, none of which is auto-nomous and all of which interact, and draw attention to the often neglected fact that the 'middle class commercial' and academic strands of culture are not identical![9] Moreover, Chanan and Gilchrist (1974, p. 32) expose the dangers of a simple dichotomisation into middle-class and working-class cultures, while at the same time gently ridiculing this kind of approach:

> The attempt to list features of authentic working class culture such as brass bands, pigeon-fancying, pubs and football, though it does draw our attention to entire aspects of life which we tend to under-value or ignore, is faintly absurd, inviting the wrong sorts of con-clusion, as if these were the working class answer to Shakespeare, Beethoven and Michelangelo.

For present purposes, it is important to note that the linguistic variability hypothesis does not require a parallel cultural variability hypothesis. It is unfortunate that Levitas (1976), in his critique of the latter, also appears to reject the former and, with it, *all* 'difference theories'. His attack on Labov (1969) and Ginsburg (1972) is un-necessary. While it is true that Labov (1969) is often cited in support of community-based curricula and theories of cultural variation, in Britain the cultural variability hypothesis has a much longer history, going back at least to Hoggart (1957). Moreover, rejection of the verbal deficit theory does not logically entail rejection of all forms of positive educational (and other) intervention in favour of those who are socially and economically deprived; nor does it imply any case against the provision of free nursery schooling. It is hoped that this brief digression will have gone some way towards clearing up certain widespread misunderstandings about the educational implications of the linguistic variability hypothesis.

Without doubt, the most important direct reaction to the verbal deficit theory has been the development of the linguistic variability hypothesis, as well as criticism of the deficit theory. Over and above this there have been a number of significant developments, which in some cases seem to have arisen in a more diffuse way from the sheer interest in language and education generated by the deficit theory and the controversies surrounding it. One of the most valuable such developments has been a growing interest in the actual use of language in the classroom, based on actual observation of classroom behaviour. In Britain the pioneer work in this area is Barnes *et al.* (1971), which was first published in 1969. Some work on language in the classroom has been undertaken from a primarily sociolinguistic perspective, for example, Sinclair and Coulthard (1975), Stubbs (1976a, pp. 68—117), while other work has tended to start from an interactionalist approach. Examples of the latter include Barnes (1973), Boydell (1975), Stubbs (1975 and 1976b), Belcourt and Gordon (1980) and — perhaps most outstanding of all — Delamont (1976). In many cases the two perspectives merge, almost imperceptibly. Sinclair and Coulthard (1975) are concerned in the first instance with discourse analysis, yet their categories are entirely interactionalist: if not interpreted in this way their taxonomy would be arbitrary. It emerged very early in work on language in the classroom that there are many unstated rules governing pupil-teacher interaction in classrooms, irrespective of whether a school is 'traditional' or in some sense 'progressive'. Later work has tended to concentrate more on the implicit meanings, verbal and non-verbal, conveyed by classroom interaction.[10]

In Britain the verbal deficit theory won considerable support among educationalists in the late 1960s and the 1970s. The Newsom Report (1963, p. 15), which was concerned with the 'education of pupils aged 13 to 16 of average and less than average ability', had already endorsed a variant of the verbal deficit theory.

There is a gulf between those who have, and the many who have not, sufficient command of words to be able to listen and discuss rationally; to express ideas and feelings clearly; and even to have any ideas at all. We simply do not know how many people are frustrated in their lives by inability ever to express themselves adequately; or how many never develop intellectually because they lack the words with which to think and to reason . . .

The evidence of research increasingly suggests that linguistic inadequacy, disadvantages in social and physical background, and poor attainments in school, are closely associated. Because the forms of speech which are all they ever require for daily use in their homes and the neighbourhoods in which they live are restricted, some boys and girls may never acquire the basic means of learning and their intellectual potential is therefore masked.

The verbal deficit theory also received favourable comment in the Plowden Report (1967, Vol. 1, p. 119). The Bullock Report (1975, pp. 52–73) treats the theory as largely unproblematical and takes its main tenets for granted. There is only one brief reference to American criticisms of the theory, and that consists of a perfunctory paragraph on Labov (1969). Between the publication of these two reports Bernstein's theories were popularised by Lawton (1968) and Lee (1973), and a large number of brief and almost entirely uncritical popularisations appeared in a wide range of other books on education, notably in King (1969), Banks (1971), Herriot (1971), Wilkinson (1971) and Roberts (1972). During the same period more general deficit theories were also popularised by Creber (1972) and Doughty and Thornton (1973). Moreover, in 1973 the Schools Council project, *Communication Skills in Early Childhood* was launched under the direction of Joan Tough. In this project Bernstein's dichotomy is replaced by a complex series of continua, ranging in practice from high to low usage. Her basic position as a deficit theorist emerges clearly in Tough (1976, p. 4):

The Preschool Education Project recognized that teachers need more knowledge about the characteristics of disadvantage in early childhood, particularly about children's early learning in the home, and the role of the language experience in the learning process. It called for an examination of alternative approaches to the promotion of language skills in young children in school and appealed for help for teachers, so that they might develop skill in recognizing children's problems in using language.

In outline, Tough's ultimate goal is to discover the key characteristics of the language-use of 'advantaged' children, so that 'disadvantaged' children can be taught those linguistic skills which the former already possess, or acquire spontaneously. But it is apparent from Tough (1976, pp. 37–9) that every child is seen as a potential linguistic problem, if only on a minor scale, and not surprisingly she suggests that teachers should monitor and keep detailed records of the linguistic development of all children in the Infant School by use of sampling techniques. Here the social pathology or social administration model underlying all verbal deficit theories is taken to its logical – and unmanageable – conclusion.

Apart from a few criticisms in Lawton (1968) and the publication of Coulthard (1969), Keddie (1972) and of the first edition of Rosen (1974) in 1972, British educationalists and linguists were slow to attack the verbal deficit theory. By the mid-1970s it looked as if Bernstein's theory had attained the status of educational orthodoxy. Medlicott (1975, p. 575) wrote somewhat ironically of 'Bernstein, without a smattering of whose theories no young teacher could be considered trained'. Rogers (1976, p. 20) wrote, with some sense of alarm, that: 'The almost religious fervour with which the work of Bernstein is associated has tended to lead to a generation of newly trained teachers with a veneration of his work hardly matched by their understanding of it.'

But the mid-1970s also saw the publication of Jackson (1974), Trudgill (1975), Dittmar (1976) and Stubbs (1976a), all of which criticise Bernstein. In addition, Wells (1977) provided a highly sceptical review of Tough (1977). Although these critical writings, together with the increased dissemination of Britain of some American attacks on the verbal deficit theory, have gone some way towards redressing the balance, at least on an academic level, it is difficult to assess to what extent the theory is accepted by administrators, policy-makers, educationalists and teachers. In 1977 the present author conducted a small-scale research project to investigate the reception of Bernstein's theory among primary school teachers. The survey was based on interviews with a self-selecting sample of twenty teachers and, of these, fifteen were at least broadly sympathetic to Bernstein's theory.[11] In view of the size and nature of the sample and the methodology employed, considerable caution is needed in interpreting the findings. Teachers who had only a 'casual' degree of acquaintance with the theory were, without exception, in sympathy with it. On the other hand, the findings did not bear out the depressing view expressed by Rogers, quoted above. It can safely be asserted that

in Britain verbal deficit theories do not enjoy anything like the hold
once exercised by the psychometric intelligence theory.[12]

Notes

1.   Efforts to obtain a copy of Lazar and Darlington (1978) failed and the
author is much indebted to Professor A.D.B. Clarke, of the University of Hull, for
a copy of the latter's abstract of the report.
2.   See Trudgill (1974, pp. 13–23 and 64–83).
3.   The transformational generative school of linguistics has been criticised
for allegedly treating an idealised version of the language as absolute. However, it
is clear from Chomsky (1965, p. 3) that he regards idealisation as little or no
more than a prerequisite for linguistic theory and in no sense as a prescription for
individual speakers:

> Linguistic theory is concerned primarily with an ideal speaker-listener, in a
> completely homogeneous speech-community, who knows its language per-
> fectly and is unaffected by such grammatically irrelevant conditions as
> memory limitations, distractions, shifts of attention and interest, and errors
> (random or characteristic) in applying his knowledge of the language in actual
> performance.

This had the inevitable effect of narrowing the scope of theoretical linguistics
and divorcing it from language as actually spoken. This point is raised by Mitsou
Ronat in an interview with Chomsky, reproduced in Chomsky (1979, p. 57):

> M.R.: Certain sociologists accuse linguistics of participating in the
> legitimation of the dominant language [dialect – JCBG] ... But above all, they
> reproach linguistics for its idealization, which removes it from social reality.
> N.C.: Opposition to idealization is simply objection to rationality; it amounts
> to nothing more than an insistence that we shall not have meaningful
> intellectual work. Phenomena that are complicated enough to be worth
> studying generally involve the interaction of several systems. Therefore you
> *must* abstract some object of study, you must eliminate those factors which
> are not pertinent. At least if you want to conduct an investigation which is
> not trivial. In the natural sciences this isn't even discussed, it is self-evident.
> In the human sciences, people continue to question it. That is unfortunate.
> (Chomsky's italics)

It can however be argued that this view plays into the hands of those who take a
monolithic view of language, however clear the real conceptions and intentions
of linguists of the transformational generative school. At the same time
linguistic theories of this kind achieve power of generalisation at the expense of
narrowing their base. Many linguists feel that the base is so narrow as to under-
mine the value of such theories. After all, what is one to make of a theory that
can make impressive generalisations about an idealisation, but is hardly in a
position to say much about every-day conversational speech? Nor is it surprising
that some should see in the transformational generative school little more than a
brilliant, highly sophisticated continuation of the standard text-book grammar
tradition. On the other hand, the efforts of those who take speech as their
starting-point have, at least until very recently, been bedevilled by the sheer
difficulty (once outside the realms of phonetics and phonology) of establishing a

system of generalisations. At present the conflict between the two lines of approach constitutes the most fundamental controversy of all within linguistics.

4.   In general terms the history of the majority of Negro dialects spoken in the USA appears, on the basis of the best evidence now available, to be as follows. On arrival in America the Negro slaves spoke their own African languages, but soon had to learn English. Since, with only a handful of exceptions, no attempt was made to teach them English and since moreover direct contact with whites was usually very limited, the vast majority of Negroes acquired a pidginised variety of the dialects of English spoken in the Southern States and spoke this in addition to their own languages. In the course of a few generations the African languages ceased to be spoken in America, the pidginised varieties of English became the sole language of the American Negroes, thus acquiring the status of creole(s). Gradually, in the eighteenth century, the creole(s) came to approximate increasingly to standard English – much more quickly among Negro slaves in domestic service than among those used for agricultural labour. With mass migration to the Northern States after the Civil War, the process of approximation accelerated rapidly. In the South, compulsory schooling even with strict racial segregation, and increased access to mass media of communication, especially in the present century, has also led to a greatly increased degree of approximation to the standard. Several questions still await definitive answers. For example, did the now extinct creole(s) incorporate syntactic features of African languages and, if so, do any of these still survive in the Negro dialects? What, exactly, happened in those parts of the USA where the Negroes once spoke French-based or Spanish-based creole(s), and have any features of the latter survived in the Negro dialects spoken in the regions in question?

The above refers to Negro dialects in the USA. In the West Indies and in Britain the Negro dialects have developed on somewhat different lines, though there are similarities. Much of the research in this field is conceived within a broad, Carribean framework, as exemplified in Whitten and Szwed (eds., 1970), rather than in a purely North American context.

The present author wishes to stress, with Stewart (1970, p. 357n5): 'In referring to types of languages, linguists use the terms *pidgin* and *creole* in a technical sense which has none of the derogatory or racial connotations of popular uses of these terms.'

5.   From a personal communication (Dr M.W. Stubbs to JCBG, 20 September 1977).

6.   See Stubbs (1980, pp. 132–5).

7.   Figures given by Trudgill in a 'question-and-answer' session following a lecture given (by himself) at the University of East Anglia, 27 January 1978.

8.   See, for example, the comments made at a conference by Freeman (1973, pp. 9–10) on this last point:

> Despite heroic efforts by truly dedicated teachers it has proved increasingly difficult to achieve any success with less able children who, supposedly, reach a 'linguistic ceiling' by the end of the third year if not earlier. The question is posed: 'What can we do with those pupils who are not capable of doing 'O' level or even CSE language but who are still timetabled for French?' The answer is found in the establishment of courses in which background becomes foreground and language learning is limited to a 'survival kit.'

9.   Chanan and Gilchrist (1974, p. 32) note: 'We may discern at least five strands in culture: working class as such (e.g. trade unionism); regional; popular (in the mass media sense); middle class commercial; and academic.' When considering an ethnic minority living in an urban ghetto one would have to add a

specifically ethnic strand.

10. This discussion of language in the classroom is no more than a thumb-nail sketch. For more detail, readers should consult the various writings mentioned, in particular Stubbs (1976a, pp. 68–117) and Delamont (1976). See also the collectaneous works Chanan and Delamont (eds., 1975) and Stubbs and Delamont (eds., 1976).

11. See Gordon (1978b) for details of the project and the findings. Beyond this one has to rely on anecdotal evidence. The experiences of a recent graduate of the University of East Anglia provide an excellent illustration of widely divergent attitudes to (and types of reception of) verbal deficit theories. After graduating in 1978, Miss Judith Middleton did a PGCE course at the University of Leicester (1978–9). In the taught part of the course, deficit theories – and especially that of Basil Bernstein – were examined very critically and, as she said, 'torn to shreds'. As part of her course, she also paid a number of visits to local schools (over and above her teaching practice). In connection with one such visit she wrote:

> A week ago our group visited a Junior School on a very poor council estate. It is a very rough area and the whole thing has been a terrible planning blunder. As a result *all* of the pupils at this Junior School are 'disadvantaged.' The headmaster came out with the classic statement that 'These children have no language. Therefore they cannot think: they cannot form concepts.'
>
> I think it is going to take quite some time to dispel some of those kinds of beliefs. (From a personal communication: Miss J.E. Middleton to JCBG, 24 May 1979.)

12. In the Federal Republic of Germany, however, it seems that the Bernstein-Oevermann variant of the verbal deficit theory *does* at present enjoy a position of virtual hegemony as an explanation of the uneven social distribution of educational attainment.

5   VERBAL DEFICIT THEORIES IN CONTEXT

At the end of Chapter 1 attention was drawn to the fact that when Bernstein's first paper advancing a verbal deficit theory was originally published in 1958 this kind of theory was not entirely new; the point was illustrated in Chapter 2 by a quotation from the Newbolt Report (1921) which encapsulated most of the main tenets of the classical version of the theory. In less strident tones the Hadow Report (1931, p. 56) also outlined a somewhat more sophisticated theory of verbal and cultural deficit:

> In the poor home it is the linguistic and literary side of the child's mental equipment that suffers most. His vocabulary is limited; his general knowledge is narrow; he has little opportunity for reading, and his power of expressing himself in good English is inadequate . . . In the household where the family is small and means are adequate the child usually enters school with the foundations of education already well laid . . . For many young children from the poorest homes all this is reversed. Their parents know very little of any life except their own, and have neither the time nor the leisure to impart what little they know. The vocabulary that the child picks up is restricted to a few hundred words, most of them inaccurate, uncouth, and mispronounced, and a good many of them unfit for reproduction in the classroom. There is no literature that deserves the title, and the pictures are equally unworthy of their name. His universe is closed in and circumscribed by walls of brick and a pall of smoke.

However, this cultural and linguistic explanation for class-linked differences in readiness for school, and implicitly also in initial educability, is mentioned only in passing in the Report and does not form the basis of any conclusions drawn or recommendations made in the Report.[1] Indeed, given that the sociological study of education was virtually unknown in Britain at that time, it is difficult to see how the Consultative Committee (which compiled the Report) could have taken these comments much further, even if it had wished to do so. Why did the verbal deficit theory achieve prominence in educational thinking when it did? The question is not why Bernstein began advancing his theory in and after 1958 but: Why were versions of the deficit theory so widely and even enthusiastically received in the 1960s and 1970s in Britain, America and some other countries? The discussion below focuses on the situation in Britain, but relevant circumstances in America are also touched upon briefly.

Mention has already been made of the prolonged boom between 1940 and 1973 and the growing demand for skilled manpower.[2] During the Second World War Britain attained a remarkably high degree of economic co-ordination in furtherance of the overall prosecution of the war and in order to lay foundations for post-war reconstruction. Increasingly, *people* — and their abilities, skills, training, health, welfare and education — came to be seen as a valuable and scarce national resource. The view that human ability and its systematic development are a public asset, and that failure to educate all to the maximum of their potential is a form of social waste, was not novel[3] but previously this had been very much a minority view which had found expression only sporadically. (Earlier demands from the Labour Movement for secondary education for all and for easier access to further and higher education had generally argued for equality of opportunity and had stressed the case for treating secondary education as a basic right, rather than the concept of education as a form of national investment.) In the Second World War there was a sudden and profound change of attitude reflecting an even more sudden and drastic change in circumstances. The new attitude towards people, towards human potential, was in marked contrast to the prevailing attitudes and realities of the interwar depression. As Jordan (1943, p. 48) observed at the time:

> In 1931 every adult was a possible applicant for unemployment pay, in 1943 he is so valuable that he can no longer be allowed to order his own industrial destiny or pursue his own individual purposes. The future trend of events will . . . endow the nation's children with a like scarcity value. We shall then provide education, not because it is socially expedient, but because it is a national necessity.

Although Jordan's predictions about the future were based in part on mistaken assumptions about the post-war birth-rate, his statement provides an accurate reflection of prevailing attitudes in Britain at the time and in general terms his prediction turned out to be correct. Contrary to widespread fears, the end of the war was not followed by a slump but by a steady rise in output. Moreover, despite an upsurge

in the birth-rate from 1944 to 1949, the view that manpower — both
present and future — was a scarce national asset persisted for about
another quarter of a century, and with it the view that adequate
educational provision was a matter of considerable public importance.
It should be stressed, however, that there was no neat or exact correspondence between the state of the economy and the expansion and
reorganisation of the education system. In particular, the 1950s were
characterised by a high degree of inactivity in this field on the part of
the central government, and local initiatives during this decade were, on
the whole, limited in scope. In the event, the greatest period of change
in education in the post-war period — the large-scale expansion of
higher education, widespread comprehensive reorganisation and the
raising of the minimum school-leaving age to 16 — was in the 1960s
and early 1970s and thus overlapped with a series of economic crises in
the mid- and late 1960s which, viewed in retrospect, foreshadowed the
onset of the depression in and after 1973. Thus there was a considerable
time-lag in the adaptation of the education system to the needs of the
economy.

The war-time view of human beings as an asset and of their education
as an investment found perhaps its clearest expression in the White
Paper, *Educational Reconstruction* (1943), which formed the immediate basis for many of the provisions of the 1944 Education Act.
On the first page of the text, immediately under the title, stands as an
epigraph the (unascribed) quotation 'Upon the education of the people
of this country the fate of this country depends'. A little later
Educational Reconstruction (1943, p. 1) states:

> In the youth of the nation we have our greatest national asset.
> Even on a basis of mere expediency we cannot afford not to
> develop this asset to the greatest advantage. It is the object of
> the present proposals to strengthen and inspire the younger
> generation. For it is as true to-day, as when it was first said, that
> 'the bulwarks of a city are its men.'
> [. . .] With these ends in view the Government propose to
> recast the national education service.

Although the specifically reconstructionalist rhetoric of the 1940s
disappeared, this kind of thinking, in various different forms,
dominated all major official reports on education, training and related
matters up to and including the Plowden Report (1967) and beyond.
Not surprisingly, the same kind of thinking predominated in most

non-official writings on educational planning. Although there were, of course, challenges from private quarters, these attracted relatively little public notice till the publication, by the *Critical Quarterly*, of *Black Papers* 1 and 2 in 1969.[4] The greatest monument to the concept of human potential as an asset and of education as public investment was the Robbins Report (1963) on higher education. Although some of its economic arguments were optimistic, even specious, it set out the general case more systematically and thoroughly than any other official report published since the war. There is of course a corollary to this view of human potential and education. Government investment in education can easily degenerate into crude attempts at manpower planning. This becomes particularly evident during a depression when, to some extent at least, human potential ceases to be seen as the scarce asset that it constitutes during a boom, and manpower planning is used as a justification for making savings in educational expenditure and reductions in actual provision.[5]

Of the various official reports that appeared in the post-war period, there is one that is of particular interest in connection with the rise and reception of the verbal deficit theory, namely *Early Leaving* (1954). This report, by the Central Advisory Council for Education (England), investigated the phenomenon of 'early leaving' from grammar schools. The concept posed certain problems from the outset. In the early 1950s the idea that a grammar school course should normally culminate for nearly all its pupils in two or more 'A' level passes was not firmly established. In many parts of the country the grammar schools were the only educational establishments in the public sector providing schooling beyond the minimum statutory school-leaving age of 15, and thus the only schools at which any kind of leaving certificate could be obtained. In other words, the grammar schools in many cases existed to serve a dual function: first, to cater for pupils intending to stay in full-time education till 18+ and hoping to leave with two or more 'A' level passes; secondly, to provide for pupils intending to leave at 16+, usually with about four or more 'O' level passes. (Of course, it was not the case that all grammar schools catered equally for these two groups. Especially in conurbations there was a tendency for individual grammar schools to cater predominantly for one rather than the other category, and more generally there was a distinct rank-order among the various grammar schools in any one area.) As the restrictions on the minimum age at which candidates could be presented for public examinations were relaxed after 1952 and it thus became possible to take these

examinations in secondary modern schools,[6] the view increasingly
gained ground that the primary, if not sole, function of the grammar
school was to provide for the former category of pupils. For example,
Floud *et al.* (1957, p. 116) distinguish between *premature* leavers,
'who leave as soon as they are legally able or shortly after', and *early*
leavers, 'who stay at school until the end of the five-year course (i.e.
usually until 16), but do not enter the sixth form'. Implicit in this
distinction and this terminology is the view that those who successfully
complete the five-year course, but do not proceed to the sixth form,
constitute in some sense a form of educational waste. However, *Early
Leaving* (1954, pp. 1–3) readily accepted the dual function of the
grammar school, though it expressed disquiet about the large number
of 'lost sixth formers'.[7]

Working on the basis of the 1946 intake at a representative sample
of just under 10 per cent of the 1,217 grammar schools in England[8]
at that time (1953?), the report found that only 24.1 per cent of the
original intake had successfully completed a sixth-form course or were
still at school in 1953. Even more alarming was the fact that 18.8 per
cent had left before completing a five-year course and a further 19.0
per cent who had stayed for five years had failed to obtain even three
GCE passes at Ordinary level. These two groups constituted
educational waste on a massive scale. Closer inspection revealed that
a very high proportion of these early leavers and failures came from
the semi-skilled and unskilled strata. The report does not give the
exact proportion. However, *Early Leaving* (1954, p. 34) estimates
that the 1946 grammar school intake in England contained about
16,000 children from these strata and notes:

> Our sample tells us . . . that of approximately 16,000 children
> who in 1946 entered grammar schools throughout England from
> such homes, about 9,000 failed to get three passes at Ordinary
> level, and of these about 5,000 left before the end of the fifth
> year.

Clearly, this phenomenon called for some explanation. The report
considered a variety of possible factors, including the most obvious
forms of social and economic disadvantage, such as poor housing and
financial problems; but attention tended to focus on 'the influence
of the home', including such things as parental and peer-group
attitudes towards education *versus* early paid employment. However,
throughout the report the compilers seem baffled by nearly everything

that they describe.[9] This is especially clear in their attempts to account
for the high proportion of early and premature leavers from the semi-
skilled and unskilled strata and, above all, in the discussion of the
influence of the home environment. At this point the report confesses
almost complete ignorance. In this connection *Early Leaving* (1954,
p. 35) states:

> Throughout our consideration of this problem we felt ourselves, in
> spite of much public discussion, to be in territory that had so far
> been little explored; and it is probable that many economic, social
> and perhaps biological factors have escaped us. We are here in a field
> where many inhibitory influences are at work, often in an obscure
> manner. Educational sub-normality in parents [!] may play a part . . .

The report went on to appeal for further research into this whole area.
The need for an answer to the question was urgent, for as the Minister
of Education, David Eccles, remarked in his Foreword to *Early Leaving*
(1954, p. v):

> Now that our manpower is fully stretched and the demand for
> trained men and women exceeds the supply everyone can see the
> importance, if our standard of life is to be raised, of developing to
> the full all the talent we have.

Five years later the Crowther Report (1959) returned to the problem
of educational waste resulting from early and premature leaving –
and this time not only in grammar schools, but throughout the whole
school system. It concluded that the most effective remedy was to
raise the minimum statutory school-leaving age to 16.[10] The report also
commented tentatively on wastage due to the lack of sufficient
university places for suitably qualified applicants, although this fell
outside its terms of reference.[11]

Directly, and more often indirectly, the question of securing
sufficient skilled and qualified manpower came to dominate the
sociology of education in the 1950s, and remained a major preoccupation for much of the following decade and beyond. Official
publications tended to discuss the issue directly and openly; but in
much of the non-official literature the emphasis lay more on the means
of securing equality of opportunity. Yet underlying many of the
egalitarian arguments presented in such works as Glass (ed., 1954),
Floud *et al.* (1957), Douglas (1964) and also, for that matter, the

Robbins Report (1963), was the assumption that if the overall level of educational provision were increased, improved and made structurally less rigid, this would achieve two objectives simultaneously. First, a greater degree of equality of opportunity would be secured and secondly, there would be a reasonable likelihood that the manpower problem would be solved. To say this is not to disvalue the egalitarian aspects of these publications, but to put them into context. Without the manpower problem it is unlikely that pressures for egalitarian change from other quarters, notably the Labour Movement, would have had much impact on government policy. (During the interwar depression such demands from the Labour Movement met with relatively little success.)

One important theoretical problem remained largely unresolved — namely, a coherent explanation for the uneven social distribution of educational attainment and, more specifically, an explanation for the high concentration of educational waste, failure and under achievement among children from the semi-skilled and unskilled strata. By the late 1950s all the more obvious material factors and also some relevant subcultural influences had been identified. Floud *et al.* (1957, p. 114) had concluded, on the basis of a geographically limited but very thorough survey: 'It has now been established beyond doubt that there is a process of social as well as academic selection at work in the schools.' Though Floud and her collaborators had established many specific factors, they remained largely discrete and the precise nature of this process of social selection remained largely obscure. In short, what was lacking was a general, overarching theory. Whether such a theory was strictly necessary is open to question, but if a theory of this kind could be formulated it might ultimately provide a key to solving the related problems of manpower shortages, inequality of opportunity and the relatively high level of educational under achievement and waste among children from the lower working classes.

Such were the preoccupations, and such was the climate, within the sociology of education when Bernstein's first papers were published in and after 1958. In retrospect, it is clear that a problem had arisen from the fact that the sociology of education had sought to explain the uneven social distribution of educational attainment without having a general theory to account for differential educational attainment as such (without reference to social class). This is not surprising. Confidence in the psychometric intelligence theory had been shaken. Quite apart from the critique provided by Simon (1953), there was now a wealth of statistical information, not least in *Early Leaving* (1954) and the Crowther Report (1959), which showed that intelligence test were a poor predictor of longer-term educational success; and some psychometrists were now making a particular point of stressing that intelligence was a necessary, but not sufficient, condition for academic success.[12] However, no alternative theory had yet been formulated in any great detail. There was therefore a theoretical and ideological vacuum, which in the course of the 1960s came to be filled, especially for many sociologists and educationalists, by Bernstein's theory on language, social class, family types and education. Rosen (1974, p. 3) comments: 'Whereas in the fifties children had their IQs branded on their forehead, in the sixties more and more of them had the brand changed to "restricted" or "elaborated." The ideology vacuum had been filled.'

Rosen's statement requires some qualification and amplification. It should be noted that, as far as is known, secondary selection has never been carried out in this country on the basis of the labels *restricted* and *elaborated* code, though one cannot exclude the possibility that they may conceivably have played a subsidiary role in the process in some cases, for example, if used in headteachers' recommendations. This point is, however, relatively minor. When an ideology vacuum of the kind described occurs it cannot be filled by *any* theory. In order to fill such a gap a theory must fulfil certain conditions. Above all, it can only succeed in this role if it incorporates or builds on existing notions and theories, and this is what Bernstein's theory does.

The most immediately striking feature of Bernstein's theory is its environmentalism (though he does not actually express rejection of the psychometric intelligence theory). In itself, this emphasis on environment was not new in 1958, and had become increasingly central to the sociology of education in Britain as it had evolved in the 1940s and 1950s. Bernstein's environmentalism seems to offer the very antithesis to the psychometric intelligence theory with its overriding emphasis on heredity. Yet on closer scrutiny it is apparent that there is no clear-cut antithesis between the two theories. Both are essentially deterministic and hold that when children embark on their statutory schooling they already differ markedly in terms of educability. For Bernstein, the social structure, acting via class-linked family-types, limits and largely determines access to elaborated code, which alone provides the key to universalistic meanings — the real stuff of school education, at least beyond the infant stage. This determinism is not a necessary corollary of deficit theories. For example, if one rejected the view that the early years of the child's development (up to, say, age 5) are of decisive significance in influencing the individual's future development, any deficit of the kind postulated by Bernstein might easily be made good later; but Bernstein does not depart from psychological orthodoxy on this point.[13] Or, in view of the *linguistic* determinism of the deficit theory, one might argue in favour of pre-school compensatory linguistic education, as do the proponents of the classical version of the verbal deficit theory, but nowhere does Bernstein suggest this and he expressly rejects it in Bernstein (1969). His theory, as it stands, is no less deterministic than the psychometric intelligence theory. His determinism comes out clearly in a passage in Bernstein (1970, p. 143):

> I am suggesting that if we look into the work relationships of this particular group [the lower working class], its community relation-ships, its family role systems, it is reasonable to argue that the genes of social class may well be carried less through a genetic code, but far more through a communication code that social class itself promotes.

Nor do the affinities between the two theories end with the matter of cognitive and educational determinism. The psychometric intelligence theory and all versions of the verbal deficit theory (not just Bernstein's) share the assumption that there is in some sense one overriding phenomenon governing educability. In the case of the one theory, it is intelligence; in the other, it is speech. Most verbal deficit theories include subordinate concepts of cultural deficit, but in this respect there are also similarities between the two theories. All more modern versions of the psychometric intelligence theory see intelligence as multiplex, as made up of different kinds of intelligence (for example, verbal, mathematical, visuo-spatial), but they are all treated as com-ponents of one superordinate phenomenon — intelligence. There is also another resemblance which, though perhaps fortuitous, deserves mention. Ever since the formulation of the Galtonian paradigm in 1869, psychometrists have repeatedly failed to provide a satisfactory definition of intelligence. Similarly, as noted in Chapter 3, in Bernstein's theory the central concept, namely that of the socio-linguistic codes, is never defined satisfactorily. The persistent failures in the case of both theories to provide satisfactory definitions raises serious doubts as to whether either intelligence or the codes have any real existence at all. On present evidence both are mere reifications. (Much the same problem arises in a slightly different form in the classical verbal deficit theory. In this version language or speech are treated as determinants of cognitive development, but the exact nature of the relationship is left largely undiscussed. And such discussion as is offered is based on unreliable observation of speech, pure speculation or Whorfian metaphysics.) Thus both the verbal deficit theory and the psychometric intelligence theory operate with central concepts grounded in philosophical idealism rather than science.

In addition to these affinities, there are also further links between Bernstein's theory and assumptions which were fairly common in educational thought in the 1950s. Even towards the end of the decade the Norwood ideology of 'types of mind' was still widespread. Ellen Wilkinson (Minister of Education, 1945–7) had adopted this ideology and given it enthusiastic expression in the Ministry of Education Pamphlet No. 9, *The New Secondary Education* (1947), which was reprinted as late as 1958, despite criticism of both the Norwood Report and the pamphlet.[14] It would be hard to imagine a more drastic restatement of the types of mind ideology than Bernstein (1958), though he postulates two, not three, kinds. In this paper he argues that in general lower working-class children are perceptually sensitive only to content, while others are sensitive to structure as well as content. Although he does not express this view again, nearly all his subsequent papers on language, social class and education are characterised by a dichotomisation of the school-population into the linguistic and cognitive 'haves' and 'have-nots'. Of course, the latter are now seen as a minority, but in this modified form the types of mind ideology persisted in the 1970s.

 Finally, Bernstein's ideas, especially as expressed in his first two papers, accorded closely with prevailing normative attitudes towards language and also with deep-seated stereotyped views of lower working-class speech and life-styles. In the 1950s normative or prescriptivist attitudes towards language were still widespread among teachers and educationalists (and the general public). A brief digression may serve to illustrate this. The last edition of the Board of Education's *Handbook of Suggestions for the Consideration of Teachers . . .* (1937, pp. 377–8) had made out a case for a policy of bi-dialectalism.[15] Although the argument was somewhat muddled, the general intention was clear. The *Handbook* was not revised after 1937, though reprints continued to be published until 1948. It was largely superseded by official pamphlets on a range of topics, including specific subjects in the school curriculum. The Ministry of Education Pamphlet No. 26, *Language: Some Suggestions for Teachers of English . . .* (1954, pp. 77–8) expressed a general preference for tolerance of linguistic diversity:

> The problem of *dialect* or *regional speech* is perhaps not as difficult as is sometimes supposed. If the same social tolerance were extended to good examples of regional English as to good examples of educated Scots and Irish, no great harm would come to the English language and many people's lives would be easier. The reverse requirement of such a tolerance is that English, of whatever regional flavour, should be as free from mumbling and from mangled vowels and missing consonants as is educated Scots or Irish and that its cadence should be as agreeable as that of the English spoken in, say, Cardiganshire. If the language is audibly uttered, if the consonants are given full force, if uncouth provincialisms of vocabulary are eliminated and if the intonation is pleasantly modulated, there are few regions of England (though there are some) that have not their own agreeable and acceptable varieties of English.
>
> A cautious and exacting tolerance of this kind might be a sounder policy than the 'bilingualism' which is often advocated as the only possible compromise between dialect and 'standard' English. Gladstone retained the northern vowels and Tennyson spoke broad Lincolnshire to the end of his days.

Much might be said from the standpoint of linguistics about this passage, which in 1954 represented something of an avant-garde point of view, not only in official thinking. Quite apart from the failure to distinguish between accent and dialect, the argument is confused. For example, the reader is told that there are some regions of England which do not have 'their own . . . acceptable varieties of English', but they are not specified. In order to be acceptable (to whom?) an accent (or dialect?) must apparently be free of 'uncouth provincialisms of vocabulary', its intonation must be 'pleasantly modulated', and, ideally, its use should have been dignified by an eminent Victorian! The whole line of argument is characterised by aestheticism, carried to the point of a cult, and by irrational and irrelevant value-judgements. The plea for tolerance is argued and expressed in terms which are themselves scarcely tolerant. If the exhortation had little effect, and intolerance and prescriptivist attitudes remained for a long time the norm among teachers and educationalists, this is hardly surprising, for the pamphlet itself is prescriptivist and intolerant. In fact,

Language: Some Suggestions . . . (1954) had failed to make a clear and decisive break with monolithic views of language, as is apparent in its demand that ' "English", literature as well as language' should be 'regarded by all in authority as the central expression of English life and culture'.[16] This failure to distinguish clearly between language, culture and literature is typical of the way in which monolithic views of language were used in Europe between about 1800 and 1950 to bolster concepts of national character and indeed nationalism itself. It comes as no surprise to find in *Language: Some Suggestions* . . . (1954, pp. 49–50) such sentiments as these:

> The French, the Welsh and the Scandinavians are not afraid to exalt their national cultures and to honour their national languages accordingly. The English have at least an equal need to recognize their own most priceless inheritance before it is seriously debased.

This kind of attitude favours normative grammar, for if there is a danger of debasement and of a priceless heritage being squandered, then preservation is obviously the order of the day; and such preservation can only be achieved, in the face of linguistic change, by prescriptivism and intolerance. When the pamphlet was last reprinted in 1966 these attitudes had been overtaken (not only in official thinking) by a new emphasis on spontaneity and creativity, as expressed in the epigone of the old *Handbook*, namely *Primary Education: Suggestions for the Consideration of Teachers* . . . (1959, pp. 140–5), which also stresses the importance to overall linguistic development of harmonious social relationships within the school. There is no mention in the book of problems of dialect or accent. However, such attitudes were still very much a minority view around 1960, though they were making headway among teachers in nursery and primary schools.

Bernstein's attempt to formulate an overarching theory to account for differences in educational attainment and its uneven social distribution in terms of language, family structures and social class constituted an essentially new theory, especially in terms of scope and detail, despite the existence of forerunners. The theory appeared to represent a radical departure but it did not fall outside the existing parameters of educational thinking around 1960. A much debated issue within psychometry, and one which had been revived in the 1950s, in particular in relation to educational attainment, had been the relative roles of heredity and environment.[17] In stressing the latter and in making the hitherto nebulous concept of environment

much more specific, Bernstein's theory remained in a general sense
within the orbit of controversies about nature *versus* nurture. The
limitations of this framework, and the extent to which his theory
remained within it, are well illustrated by the fact that both theories
are essentially deterministic. (For example, a theory reasserting the
Victorian concept of equality of educability would have rendered
this framework irrelevant.) Bernstein's theories also incorporated a
modified version of Norwood ideology. His early papers appeared at
a time when monolithic concepts of language and the irrational value-
judgements on speech which always go hand in hand with such
concepts were still widespread among educationalists (and the
general public). In this climate of opinion any theory which could
be interpreted as suggesting that the lower working classes did not or
could not speak English properly was hardly likely to meet with much
opposition in respect of its treatment of language.[18] These elements
of continuity with established modes of thinking in education, combined with the apparent hope held out by the environmental aspects
of the theory and, equally importantly, with the concern at official
level about educational waste and shortages of skilled and pro-
fessionally qualified manpower, did much to facilitate a favourable
reception for the theory.[19]

The context in which the classical verbal deficit theory arose in the
USA differed in a number of important respects from the post-war
situation in Britain. The USA also enjoyed a prolonged boom during
and after the Second World War and also experienced manpower
shortages, especially at the skilled and professional levels, during much
of this period, but the problem was not widely interpreted as one of
educational waste, at least until the 1960s.

In the USA the development of the verbal deficit theory was closely
linked with Project Headstart, which was launched in 1965 as part of
the Johnson Administration's 'War on Poverty' programme. The aim
of the programme was to integrate the poorer strata in America, and
in particular the population of the Negro urban ghettos, more fully
with the rest of American society. Behind this aim (and much of the
humanitarian rhetoric with which it was expressed) lay two more
specific objectives. First, the fuller utilisation of manpower, which
was particularly necessary at that time in view of the USA's rapidly
growing involvement in the Vietnam war; and secondly, an attempt
to counter the growing alienation of the Negro population from the
dominant values of American society. (By the time Project Headstart
was initiated there had already been a number of uprisings in some of

the Negro ghettos, and these spread and continued for the rest of the 1960s.)

Project Headstart was thus launched hastily in an atmosphere of urgency verging on panic. Given this context it is hardly surprising that many components of the Project were devised on an *ad hoc* basis, and the specifically linguistic programmes were devised almost entirely by educational psychologists who had little by way of theory on which to base their work in this field. To the extent that they concerned themselves with theoretical issues in the early stages, they relied on Schatzmann and Strauss (1955), Templin (1957), Riessmann (1962) and to some extent Bernstein's earliest papers. But in general, as already remarked, the programmes came first and the theory second. In practice, the educational psychologists concerned did not seek co-operation from linguists and relied instead on popular, 'common-sense' notions about language and its relationship to cognitive development. It soon emerged that they had uncritically incorporated a large body of folk-linguistic assumptions both in their programmes and in their subsequent attempts to provide a theoretical basis for these programmes. These weaknesses, together with the fact that linguistics itself was more developed in the USA than elsewhere, go some way towards accounting for the relative swiftness and vigour of reactions against the verbal deficit theory in the USA. Other factors included the lack of the expected, easily identifiable results from Project Headstart and active resistance by some sections of the Negro population to this particular attempt as integration.

Despite differences between the situation in Britain and the USA, it is clear that in both countries versions of the verbal deficit theory functioned as a theoretical adjunct and a practical instrument in an attempt at social engineering.[20] Of course, this does not mean that the verbal deficit theory is the only theory to have functioned in this way. Dittmar (1976, pp. 240–9) points out that the linguistic variability hypothesis has served the same function, at least in the USA, and because it is truer to the social facts of language its chances of fulfilling this function successfully are considerably greater. However, this does not mean that the linguistic variability hypothesis is condemned to serve attempts at social engineering. As indicated in Chapter 4, it also provides the most viable starting-point for an attack on folk-linguistic attitudes and assumptions, and thus forms a potential basis for a process of enlightenment and educational advance.

Notes

1. The comments made later in the Hadow Report (1931, pp. 95–6, 156–8) on the importance of 'language training' and 'speech training' and the recommendation that 'Language training should be regarded as fundamentally important . . . ' (p. 139) are not specifically linked to the passage quoted above. Interestingly, the embryonic deficit theory expressed in the Hadow Report (1931) is not echoed in the next Hadow Report (1933), which was concerned with nursery and infant schooling. On the contrary, the Hadow Report (1933, p. 122) displays a remarkable confidence in the ability of all normal children to learn:

> The child, *even if he has unhappily missed the advantages of a good home*, or a good nursery school or class, has already learnt to use his native powers over a wide field of activities and interests. He has acquired mastery of the simpler muscular movements and has begun to co-ordinate them. He has learnt to speak, and begun to build up a working vocabulary by which to express his needs. He has a general, and in some directions an intimate knowledge of his surroundings from which he has gained simple ideas about many things. All this he has acquired through personal experience and experiment in the natural course of growth . . . (Italics – JCBG)

2. See above, pp. 40–1.
3. This concept had been advanced by Lindsay (1926) and was at least implicit in Gray and Moshinsky (1935a and 1935b). Also the Hadow Report (1926, p. 44) had stated:

> . . . the growth of secondary and of central schools has revealed a wealth of ability among children attending the elementary schools, the existence of which is a ground both for confidence and for anxiety – confidence in the natural endowments of our fellow countrymen and *anxiety lest*, at the age at which the powers of the rising generation are most susceptible of cultivation and sensitive to neglect, *the nation should fail to turn to best account so precious a heritage.* (Italics – JCBG)

4. The *Black Papers* contained a wide range of different kinds of articles which collectively amounted to a generalised protest against what their authors interpreted as modernism in education. Few of the papers specifically challenged the view of education as a national investment.
5. Consistent with the manpower planning view of education, governments in the 1970s increasingly tended to exploit falls (past, present and predicted) in the birth-rate to make savings in certain areas of the education service, notably by closing several schools with low or falling rolls and by reducing the number of teachers in training, which involved the dissolution of many teacher training colleges. At the same time there were frequent exhortations in the latter half of the 1970s to adapt education to meet the needs of manufacturing industry. There was also much talk, on the one hand of allegedly illiterate and innumerate school-leavers, and at the other extreme of problems of over-qualification and of the qualifications spiral. No attempt was made to turn the fall in the birth-rate to educational advantage, for example, by reducing the size of classes.

Implicit in much of this government thinking was the assumption that the social value of education should be assessed primarily in economic terms. This attitude is well illustrated in the official publication *Educating Our Children: Four Subjects for Debate* (1977, pp. 12–14) and in the Green Paper which followed it, *Education in Schools: A Consultative Document* (1977). This contrasts sharply with government attitudes in the interwar years, when manpower planning attitudes towards education were much less widespread. In 1931 and 1932 the government imposed severe reductions in expenditure on education, but these were to some extent restored by 1935, despite a falling birth-rate.

6. In 1951 and 1952 candidates were not eligible to sit for the General Certificate of Education unless they were 16 on 1 September of the year of the examination. Until this restriction was lifted it was impossible to take the examination at secondary modern schools, except in those few offering courses beyond age 15+.

7. *Early Leaving* (1954, p. 11). See also the more general discussion on pp. 9–11 and 24.

8. In this context, this means England in the narrowest sense, excluding Monmouthshire (Gwent) as well as Wales, Scotland and Northern Ireland.

9. Despite this, *Early Leaving* (1954) is noteworthy as the first official report on any aspect of education to make a systematic attempt to answer major questions on the basis of sociological criteria.

10. The Crowther Report (1959, Vol. 1, p. 453) argued as follows:

The country is a long way from tapping all the available supply of talent by present methods . . .

It is most unlikely that this waste of talent can be remedied within a reasonable period without compulsion, because leaving at 15 is so deeply embedded in certain parts of the social structure.

11. This issue came to a head in the following year. The subject was debated in the Upper House in May 1960 upon a motion by Lord Simon of Wythenshawe calling on the government 'to appoint a committee to inquire into and report on the extent and nature of the provision of full-time education for those over the age of 18, whether in universities or other educational establishments'. Although the motion was lost, the Robbins Committee was set up by the Prime Minister in February 1961. Its brief was 'to review the pattern of full-time higher education in Great Britain and in the light of national needs and resources to advise Her Majesty's Government on what principles its long-term development should be based' (from Treasury Minute dated 8 February 1961, reproduced in the Robbins Report, 1963, Vol. 1, p. iii). The outcome was the longest and probably most thorough report on any aspect of education in Britain published this century. Moreover, the Robbins Committee's recommendations were, to a considerable extent, acted on fairly consistently by successive governments until about the mid-1970s.

12. See, for example, Eysenck (1962, pp. 22–4).

13. Clarke and Clarke (1976) show that the view that the first few years of life are decisive in determining the individual's subsequent development is not a product of modern psychology and that it extends back to Classical Antiquity. Clarke and Clarke (eds., 1976) is a very useful collection of articles which put a question-mark over many aspects of this tenet of psychological orthodoxy.

14. The Norwood Report (1943) and in particular the types of mind ideology had been criticised by Burt (1943b) and Fleming (1947 and 1948, pp. 118–40). Lady Simon of Wythenshawe (1948) and Dent (1949) had also criticised the ideology, as expressed both in the report and the pamphlet *The New Secondary Education*. The most scathing comment of all on the Norwood Report came from Curtis (1952, p. 144): 'Seldom has a more unscientific or more unscholarly attitude disgraced the report of a public committee.'

15. The previous edition of the *Handbook* (1927, pp. 74–6) had already

argued a case for bi-dialectalism. (Earlier editions had not done so explicitly.)

16. *Language: Some Suggestions* . . . (1954, p. 49).

17. See, for example, Vernon (ed., 1957).

18. See the interpretation by Wilkinson (1970, p. 137), quoted on p. 87n3.

19. Bernstein's work attracted support from the Department of Scientific and Industrial Research as early as 1960, and subsequently from other official bodies (see Bernstein 1971b, pp. 9–10).

20. At the same time the verbal deficit theory provided a convenient excuse for the failure to achieve equality of educational opportunity, since the deficit theorists argued (much as the psychometrists had done) that a large proportion of schoolchildren suffered from a mysterious cognitive blight which impaired their educability.

CONCLUSION AND PROSPECT

Among educationalists, there are some who are uneasy about the verbal deficit theory but who are reluctant to reject it altogether since they feel that it strengthens the case for nursery school provision. Nursery schooling can be adequately justified on the grounds that it provides relief for mothers, removes the child from the often stultifying confines of the family and brings forward the age at which the child begins to develop into a genuinely social being outside the family environment.

The verbal deficit theory cannot be counted as a branch of socio-linguistics and it has no good claim to a place in psychology or sociology, either. At times the critique offered in this study may have appeared harsh to some readers; yet, as Stubbs (1976a, p. 65) observes:

> It is unfortunate that one group of social scientists [sociolinguists] are now having to try and clear up some of the confusion caused by another group: unfortunate but necessary, since these are not mere debates between academics, but live issues affecting teachers and their pupils.

In practical terms, sociolinguistics points to a systematic attempt to foster a much higher degree of acceptance of linguistic diversity. A campaign with this end in view would not be an easy undertaking, and it is important that all involved in any such venture should be clear about what is really involved. What is ultimately at issue is not primarily linguistic diversity as such. After all, most teachers get a great deal of it, and in practice have to accept much of it, whether they like it or not. A far greater problem is the stereotyped judgements associated with various accents and dialects, including the standard dialect and RP. If teachers were merely to become more tolerant of linguistic diversity, but continued to judge pupils' potential to any significant extent on the basis of their speech, the only gain that could be expected would at best be a somewhat higher degree of self-confidence in self-expression on the part of pupils. Though valuable, this would in all probability soon be undermined by the teacher's covert judgements.

The real challenge for teachers is to reject the stereotyping and labelling that tends to pervade teaching at all levels, from the nursery school to the university, and that requires a return to the concept that all normal children are broadly similar in terms of educability, provided that their capacity to work and learn is not undermined by unsatisfactory material conditions, such as malnutrition or over-crowding in the home.

The challenge is a formidable one, involving tolerance of linguistic diversity (above all, in speech), the rejection of stereotyping and a very different attitude towards pupils. What would, perhaps, be most uncomfortable of all is that in accounting for differences in attainment the spotlight would move from the pupil to the teacher, his methods and training and the education system in which he operates. Inevitably, this would mean that in general education would have to become more teacher-centred. Despite all these difficulties, changes of this kind would do much to enhance the success of comprehensive schooling, and thus ultimately improve the chances of providing a worthwhile education for all.

APPENDIX 1

List of Manuals and Other Works on Education, Published c. 1835–
1915, Examined in Respect of their Position on Intelligence Theories.
For full bibliographical details, consult the Bibliography.)

Those books which subscribe to an intelligence theory, if only implicitly, are indicated by means of asterisks. The basic criterion used is
that of whether the author expresses a preference for classification on
the basis of 'ability', 'mental capacity', 'aptitude', 'individual differences'
and so forth rather than attainment and/or age. Such books are marked
with a *single* asterisk. However in some cases discussion of this matter
is confined to a mere page or two. A *double* asterisk denotes a book
which either openly subscribes to an intelligence theory or specifically
advocates mental testing. In cases where the author's position is unclear,
or where he prevaricates, a *single asterisk plus question-mark* is used.
Obviously, in some cases books do not fit neatly into these categories,
and it has been necessary to form a judgement on the basis of a variety
of criteria. It should not, however, be assumed that the absence of any
asterisk means that the author is unaware of differences in aptitude
regarded as natural or innate, merely that he does not treat them as
important for the organisation of teaching for normal pupils. Thus
reference to the problem of 'the dunce' does not attract an asterisk
unless the author proposes classification by ability for *normal* children.

The only book which attacks intelligence theories (Hayward, 1908)
is marked with a *double* dagger. Fitch (1881) expresses extreme
scepticism and his book is marked with a *single* dagger. However, it
should be noted that Fitch's scepticism is directed largely against the
work of the phrenologist, George Combe (1788–1858), and is in no
sense concerned with the Galtonian paradigm. Moreover, unlike
Hayward (1908) he devotes only two pages (pp. 425–6) to the
question of intelligence theories and their possible implications for the
organisation of education.

Date of first edition	Author and title or short title	Date of edition examined
1836	D. Stow, *The Training System* . . .	1836
1837	H. Dunn, *Popular Education* . . .	1837
1838	**I. Taylor [of Stanford Rivers], *Home Education* . . .	1842

Date of first edition	Author and title or short title	Date of edition examined
1840	S. Wilderspin, *A System for the Education of the Young*...	1840
1842	R.N. Collins, *The Teacher's Companion*...	1843
1850	S. Robins, *The Church Schoolmaster*	1850
c.1857	*J. Gill, *Introductory Text Book to School Education*...	1883
1859	W.M. Wooler, *Physiology of Education*...	1859
1861	*?J. Currie, *Principles and Practice of Common-School Education*	1878
1861	H. Spencer, *Education*...	1884
1862	W.J. Unwin, *The Primary School*...	1862
1863	R. Robinson, *Teacher's Manual*...	1869
1867	S.S. Laurie, *On Primary Instruction*...	1867
1868	T. Markby, *Practical Essays on Education*	1868
1871	G.C.T. Bartley, *Schools for the People*...	1871
1872	Anon., *Teaching and Management of Elementary Schools*...	1872
1872	F.E. Harding, *Practical Handbook of School Management*...	1877
1874	H. Calderwood, *On Teaching*...	1875
1874	W. Jolly, *The Public Schools*... *Suggestions to School Boards*...	1874
1874	C. Kingsley, *Health and Education*	1874
1879	A. Bain, *Education as a Science*	1879
1879	J.R. Blakiston, *The Teacher*...	1879
1880	National Society, *Advanced Manual of Teaching*	1880
1881	†J.G. Fitch, *Lectures on Teaching*...	1881
1883	*D. Kay, *Education and Educators*	1883
1884	*G. Collins, *Notes on School Management*	1887
1886	**J. Sully, *Teacher's Handbook of Psychology*	1897
1887	J. Runciman, *Schools and Scholars*	1887
1889	W.C. Coupland, *Mental and Moral Science Applied to Teaching*...	1889
1890	J.H. Cowham, *Principles of Oral Teaching*...	1896
1892	S.S. Laurie, *Institutes of Education*...	1892
1894	J.H. Cowham, *New School Method*...	1895
1894	*J. Landon, *Principles and Practice of Teaching*...	1894
1895	J. Gunn, *Class Teaching and Management*	1895
1896	T.A. Cox and R.F. Macdonald, *Suggestive Handbook of Practical School Method*...	1897
1896	*?A.H. Garlick, *New Manual of Method*	1907
1896	F.W. Hackwood, *Practical Method of Class Management*...	1897
1897	*?J. Adams, *Herbartian Psychology*...	1897
1898	C.I. Dodd, *Introduction to Herbartian Principles of Teaching*	1898
1898	D. Salmon, *The Art of Teaching*	1898
1899	P.A. Barnett, *Common Sense in Education and Teaching*...	1899
1900	G. Collar and C.W. Crook, *School Management and Methods of Instruction*...	1900
1902	A.C. Benson, *The Schoolmaster*...	1902

Date of first edition	Author and title or short title	Date of edition examined
1902	J.J. Findlay, *Principles of Class Teaching*	1902
1903	C.B. Ingham, *Education in Accordance with Natural Law* . . .	1903
1904(?)	J. Gunn, *The Infant School* . . .	1906
1904	A. Henderson, *Some Notes on Teaching*	1904
1904	T. Raymont, *Principles of Education*	1904
1905	*?S.E. Bray, *School Organisation*	1914
1905	R.E. Hughes, *School Training*	1905
1905	O.[J.] Lodge, *School Teaching and School Reform* . . .	1905
1905	C.M.[S.] Mason, *School Education*	1905
1906	C.I. Dodd, *The Child and the Curriculum*	1906
1908	††F.H. Hayward, *Education and the Heredity Spectre*	1908
1908	*?J.H. Wimms, *Introduction to Psychology* . . . *for Teachers*	1915
1908	**A. Wilson, *Education, Personality and Crime* . . .	1908
1911	E.[G.A.] Holmes, *What Is and What Might Be* . . .	1911
1911	*?J. Welton, *Psychology of Education*	1911
1912	*?J. Adams, *Evolution of Educational Theory*	1912
1912	J.J. Findlay, *The School* . . .	1912
1912	**F.H. Hayward, *Educational Administration* . . .	1912
1913	*?B. Dumville, *Child Mind: An Introduction to Psychology for Teachers*	1913
1913	[H.] T. Mark, *Modern Views on Education*	1913
1915	J. Welton, *What Do We Mean by Education?*	1915

In selecting books for consultation an attempt was made to include a wide range of different British books on education and educational psychology. Thus the above list includes not only manuals for practising teachers and those in training, but also most of the major works on education which appeared in the period under consideration and a number of books arguing various cases for reform: for example, Ingham (1903) and Lodge, O. (1905). The inclusion of educational 'classics' accounts for the relatively high proportion of books by prominent people in the list.

Entries will be found in the *Dictionary of National Biography* (and supplements) for the following authors: David Stow (1793–1864), Isaac Taylor [of Stanford Rivers] (1787–1865), Samuel Wilderspin (1792?–1866), the Rev. Sanderson Robins (1801–62), Herbert Spencer (1820–1903), Simon Somerville Laurie (1829–1909), Sir George Christopher Trout Bartley (1842–1910), the Rev. Charles Kingsley (1819–75), Alexander Bain (1818–1903), Sir Joshua Girling Fitch (1824–1903), Sir John Adams (1857–1934), Arthur Christopher Benson (1862–1925) and Sir Oliver Joseph Lodge (1851–1940).

Unfortunately, there exists no bibliography of Victorian manuals for teachers, and many of them are hard to trace. In some cases, too, copies are now rare, and it would appear that there was a tendency to treat them as ephemera. For example, in order to consult Jolly (1874), National Society (1880), Coupland (1889) and Gunn (1895) it proved necessary to have recourse to copyright libraries.

APPENDIX 2

A Brief Discussion of Some Samples of Children's Speech

Despite their weaknesses from a scientific point of view, verbal deficit theories represent an attempt to account for observable forms of linguistic behaviour on the part of groups of schoolchildren. One can reject the theory on grounds of scientific inadequacy and try to explain its currency in terms of climates of opinion. Though sufficient from a theoretical point of view, this kind of approach might give rise to the notion that linguists are unwilling to face up to 'uncomfortable realities'. Moreover, in the course of research into the reception of Bernstein's theory among primary school teachers (Gordon, 1978b), the present author found that many of the teachers interviewed felt that Bernstein's theory, or at least aspects of it, articulated something that they had encountered in their own experience.

What, then, are the kinds of linguistic behaviour among school-children that seem to lend credibility to the verbal deficit theory? With the notable exception of Tough (1976 and 1977), the great majority of writings which advance verbal deficit theories are character-ised by an almost complete absence of transcribed speech. Occasionally a few, short examples are offered in order to illustrate a point. Of course, many deficit theorists provide information in statistical form, showing for example how often and what percentage of children from different social strata used various linguistic structures or used speech for a range of different purposes. Such statistical information is a poor substitute for transcriptions, because the important question *What did the children actually say?* is left unanswered and the opportunity for offering alternative interpretations is drastically reduced.

Obviously, since verbal deficit theories are not open to empirical testing there can be no question of using transcriptions either to prove or disprove them. However, in order to identify and discuss the kinds of speech that might appear to lend some support to concepts of verbal deficit the present author conducted two small-scale studies and these are discussed below.

Two decisions had to be taken at the outset. First, what age-range should be investigated? Secondly, what techniques should be used to obtain the data? Verbal deficit theorists are in general particularly interested in the speech of children at the point where they begin compulsory schooling and during the following two years. In a British context this would mean the age-range 'rising five' up to about seven. As far as the possibility of investigating the speech of children in a reception class (ages rising five to rising six) was concerned, the author decided against studying the speech of children in this group since these children are often still very much involved in the task of adapting to the school environment. Moreover, children enter the reception class at the beginning of different terms in the academic year. Thus within any reception class the individual children's length of experience of school differs enormously, and generally this difference is increased by the fact that some children have previously attended nursery school (either full-time or half-time) while others have not. This pointed to a somewhat older age-group. The author therefore decided to investigate the speech of children in classes which had been in full-time attendance at school for not less than one year, and this meant in practice children in the age-range six-plus to seven-plus. Of course, it should not be assumed that among children in this age-range individual differences in the degree of acclimatisation to the school will have disappeared, but such differences are likely to be much less marked, and hence less distorting than would be the case with younger children.

The question of the choice of techniques for obtaining data was also problematical. Spontaneous speech is exceptionally difficult to record and transcribe, and does not necessarily provide a good indication of a child's general linguistic development. Generally, children in the age-range under investigation only speak relatively uninhibitedly when talking to a friend or relative (either of their own age or older) or in the course of play. As for the former kind of speech, tape-recordings can only be obtained by 'bugging' the children or by intruding on their privacy in equally undesirable ways. The alternative is to create, artificially, a situation (such as an interview) likely to elicit the kind of speech concerned. This sometimes works fairly well with younger children, but especially after starting school children often behave self-consciously in such circumstances and the interviewer has to rely heavily on questioning. If one decides to record the speech of children at play it is essential to use video-tape, as a transcription without any film showing the accompanying action generally conveys very little. Finally, simply to ask a child to talk — for example, to tell a story — is rarely successful. In view of these considerations the author decided to rely on interviews, while taking some steps to mitigate their distorting effects. To this end the author visited the two classes from which the children in the sample were drawn twice before any interviews were conducted. Each visit lasted about ninety minutes, and the author spent much of the time talking to the children in the sample. Moreover, when the interviews were conducted a teacher with whom the children were familiar was present and did much of the eliciting.[1]

The interviews provide no more than a sample of the speech of each child interviewed in a specific situation on a specific occasion and they do not provide any guide to the *general* stage of linguistic development of any of the children. In order to obtain a broader picture of a child's linguistic development one would have to use anthropological methods. Some linguists, for example Halliday (1975), have observed, recorded and analysed the linguistic development of their own children. Although this method can produce valuable results, it can only be used with very young children and becomes unmanageable as a child interacts with an increasingly wide range of people, as happens when the child begins to play outside the parental home, and later when the child goes to school. The method is well suited to the study of the actual process of language acquisition but not to comparative investigations into the speech of a larger number of children at a particular time.

In reading the transcriptions given below the reader should bear in mind the limitations of the interview as a method of eliciting speech and the fact that they do not provide a cross-section of the children's total linguistic repertoire. Moreover, the inherent limitations of conventional interviews as a means of eliciting speech from children, as illustrated by Labov (1969), must also be borne in mind.

The transcriptions all consist of extracts from the interviews, and none of the interviews is reproduced in its entirety. The aim in each case has been to extract from each interview one or more sequences of speech which will readily make sense to the reader and at the same time to provide an adequate cross-section of the kinds of speech used by each child in the interview. Some may object that this process of editing has the effect of focusing on what children can say, and ignores what they cannot do. As already noted, it is virtually impossible to obtain a full picture of a child's total linguistic development. Moreover, verbal deficit theories claim that there are certain linguistic things that some children cannot or do not do at all — not merely that they seldom do them. Thus if children occasionally speak or think in ways which according to deficit theories they cannot, that is evidence against, not for, the theories.[2]

School A is in a poor part of Inner London, School B in a much more favoured environment in the Northern Area of Suffolk. The author considered giving the parental occupations of the children interviewed but eventually decided not to do so. In the form in which they are generally recorded by schools, occupations often reveal little about the real socio-economic status of the parents. (Occupational designations such as 'engineer', 'council employee', 'civil servant' and 'consultant' are relatively uninformative.) Instead, the head-teachers were asked to estimate the proportion of children in their schools coming from owner-occupied homes. In the case of School A, the head put the figure at under 5 per cent, in the case of School B at not less than 85 per cent.

In both schools the sample was chosen by taking every nth name on the register, and the teachers felt that this produced a relatively representative cross-section of the children in the two classes concerned. In both schools, one child in the sample was too shy to be interviewed successfully, and the attempted interviews with the two children concerned have not been reproduced.

In the transcriptions R refers to the researcher — who was the present author. The other abbreviations and conventions require no explanation. Fictitious names have been substituted for those which occurred in the actual interviews.

School A

Pupil 1 (Boy, age 6;6)

     [. . .]
T: Would you like to be a teacher when you get older?
P_1:   ?
T: No. What would you like to be when you get older?
P_1:   A doctor.
T: You'd like to be a doctor? Is your brother a doctor?
P_1:   Nearly, and one's an engineer, nearly.
T: In?
P_1:   One's nearly an engineer and one's nearly a doctor.
T: So you want to be a doctor when you grow up.
     [. . .]
T: Now, how old would be your brother?
P_1:   One's twenty and one's nearly an engineer and one's sixteen and close to being a doctor.
T: I see. Does he go to college? Does he?
P_1:   One of them, one of them goes to a uni . . ., university and the

other go to college.

T: Which college does he go to — your sixteen-year-old?

P$_1$:   ?

T: You don't know, don't know the name of it? Does he go on a bus at all?

P$_1$:   Sometimes he gets on a train and sometimes walking and sometimes on a bus.

        [. . .]

T: What about Old Mother Hubbard? What happens in that story? It's a rhyme really, isn't it? We sing it as a song. What happens in that?

P$_1$:   Old Mother Hubbard tries to get her p . . . (indistinct) doggie a bone but the cupboard is empty.

T: I see.

P$_1$:   She went to the b . . . (indistinct) to get him bread but, but when she came back, the poor dog was dead.

T: That's sad, isn't it?

P$_1$:   Although she, she, she went to the barbara's. A barber.

T: What's a barber, d'you know?

P$_1$:   I can't remember. Buy him a wig.

T: Buy him a wig, yes.

P$_1$:   . . . but, but when she came back he was dancing a jig.

T: What does that mean: he was dancing a jig?

P$_1$:   I don't know.

T: You don't know? I think it's a dance, isn't it?

        [. . .]

Pupil 2 (Girl, age 7;2)

        [. . .]

T: What do you do when you first wake up?

P$_2$:   I brush my teeth.

T: You brush your teeth. When you first get up you get out of bed, brush your teeth. What happens next?

P$_2$:   I get dressed.

T: Then you get dressed. Er, d'you have a wash at all?

P$_2$:   Yes.

T: Is that before you get dressed? Or when you brush your teeth you have a wash?

P$_2$:   Before I get dressed.

T: You brush your teeth, have a wash, then you get dressed. Then what d'you do?

P₂: Put my coat on.
T: Put your coat on — and then what?
P₂: Go to school.
T: And then you come to school. You don't have any breakfast?
P₂: I do.
T: You do! You didn't tell me about breakfast. When d'you have breakfast?
P₂: In the morning.
T: In the morning. Well, what does it come after? Do you get dressed, dressed and then have breakfast?
P₂: No, I get, I get dressed, and I have my breakfast and I get my teeth brushed.
      [. . .]
T: D'you like coming to school?
P₂: Yes.
T: You do. What d'you like about school?
P₂: Eating dinner.
T: You like eating dinner, do you? D'you like doing anything else? What d'you like doing?
P₂: Doing pictures.
T: Oh, you like drawing pictures. Anything else?
T: ⌝ What sort of pictures d'you like drawing?
P₂:⌟ Writing stories.
T: Writing stories. What sort of stories d'you like?
P₂: When I went to a wedding.
T: You went to a wedding? What happened at the wedding?
P₂: I had some cake.
T: You had some cake. You like eating, don't you? Have you got lots of friends at school?
P₂: No.
T: You haven't? D'you know why that is?
P₂: No. Yes!
T: Why haven't you got lots of friends?
P₂: Because nobody's not my friend.
T: No? D'you know why?
P₂: Yes.
T: Why?
P₂: They keep on saying I stink.
T: You stink?! Well, d'you think you do?
T: ⌝
R: ⌟ No.

T: No, I don't think they're telling the truth, are they?
P₂: No.
[. . .]

Pupil 3 (Boy, age 6;3)
[. . .]
R: Now, why did I ask you not to nod and not to shake your head? . . .
P₃: (Interrupting R) Because it wouldn't come out on that and you couldn't hear it if we did. You couldn't see us and you didn't know what was happening.
R: Um. How long have you been at this school for?
P₃: Um, since a year and a little bit.
R: Yes. D'you like being at school? What d'you do at school?
P₃: (Interrupting R) We . . .
R: Sorry! D'you like being at school?
P₃: Yes.
R: Well, what d'you do at school?
P₃: Write, and things like that.
R: Things like that . . . Particular . . . ?
P₃: (Interrupting R) Fletcher[3] and there's news and things . . .
R: Did you go to another school before you came here or is this your first school?
P₃: This is my first school.
[. . .]
T: D'you know what reading-book you're on at the moment? What's it called?
P₃: *Seven. Old Dog Tom.*[4]
T: *Old Dog Tom.* What happens in *Old Dog Tom*?
P₃: They've got lots of stories about things.
T: What sort of stories? D'you know?
P₃: Er, things like *Old Dog Tom* and 'The Cat and the Mouse'.
T: Yes, that's right. D'you read at home?
P₃: Yes.
T: What sort of books d'you read at home?
P₃: Oh, some are diff . . . Most of them are different from the school ones, but some are the same.
T: I see. Does your mummy read to you?
P₃: No.
T: No?
P₃: I read to her.
T: Oh, you read to her. Does she read you a story when you go to

bed?

P₃: No.

T: No? What sort of books d'you read to your mummy then?

P₃: Um, things like . . . The only thing I do read is my reading-book.

T: Oh, you read your reading-book, do you? I thought you had other books at home. D'you go to the library?

P₃: I used to, but I don't any more.

    [. . .]

Pupil 4 (Girl, age 6;3)

    [. . .]

R: D'you like being tape-recorded? Have you ever been tape-recorded before?

P₄: Yes.

R: Now, who tape-recorded you before?

P₄: My dad.

R: Ah, your dad tape-recorded you. And how long ago was that?

P₄: Don't know.

R: You don't know. Um, d'you remember what you said? Did he play it back to you?

P₄: Yes.

    [. . .]

T: All right. D'you go home with your mummy or daddy? Have you got any brothers and sisters?

P₄: Yes.

T: What are their names?

P₄: Tommy.

T: Tommy and Lucy. Does Tommy come to school?

P₄: Yes.

T: Which school does he go to?

P₄: Here.

T: He's in the nursery, isn't he? How old is Tommy?

P₄: Three.

T: Three. Is he younger than you?

P₄: Yes.

T: And how old is Tommy, er, Lucy?

P₄: Four months.

T: Four months! She's a very little baby, isn't she? Does she come to school? What does she do all day?

P₄: She lies in bed.

T: She lies in bed. D'you know where she is now?

P₄: No.

T: No? Is she at home with mummy?

P₄: Yes.

T: Mummy looks after her?

P₄: Yes.

T: Mummy looks after her?

P₄: Yes.

T: Mummy doesn't go to work?

P₄: No.

T: No?

P₄: When I come home she goes to work.

T: Oh, your mummy goes to work when you go home . . .
    [. . .]

School B

Pupil 5 (Girl, age 7;0)

    [. . .]

T: Sally, have you, have you got any pets at home at all?

P₅: Yes.

T: Will you tell us about them?

P₅: It's two hamsters and Louise's got one and I've got one. Louise's is, Louise's has big eyes and mine has got small eyes. We think that Louise's is a girl and mine is a boy.

T: What? Because of the eyes?

P₅: Yes.

R(?): Yes.

T: Well, have they got names?

P₅: Yes.

T: Will you tell us?

P₅: Yes, mine is 'Patch', and Louise's is 'Spot'.

T: Yours is . . . ?

P₅: 'Patch'.

T: 'Patch'. And Louise's is . . . ?

P₅: 'Spots'.
    [. . .]

T: Well, before long we shall be having our holidays, won't we?

P₅: Yes.

T: What d'you look forward to in the holidays?

P₅: Going out in the garden and riding my bike.

T: In the garden?

P₅: Mm.

T: Yes.

P₅: To playing in the caravan.

T: Whereabouts is your caravan?

P₅: Near the front door.

T: And do you use your caravan during the summer at all?

P₅: Not much.

T: Do you take it out, away on holidays? D'you go away with your caravan on holiday?

P₅: We don't know yet.

T: Oh, it's a new one, is it? You haven't had it a long time.

P₅: No.

T: Yes. What would you really like to do with the caravan?

P₅: Go out on holiday.

R: Yes.

T: Anywhere you'd specially like to go?

P₅: Yes, Scotland.

T: Would you like to go to Scotland, would you? Why? Why Scotland?

P₅: Because there are . . . (indistinct) hills to play on and trees to climb up.
       [. . .]

Pupil 6 (Boy, age 6;11)

       [. . .]

T: D'you enjoy reading comics?

P₆: Yes.

T: Do you? Which comics?

P₆: There's Robin Hood I like reading and there's lots, but I can't remember.

T: You can't remember? What sort of stories d'you like in your comics?

P₆: When he goes in the forest and that piece.

T: Oh, I see, yes. Er, you usually stay for your school dinners, John, don't you?

P₆: Yes.

T: D'you like school dinners?

P₆: Yes.

T: Do you? Er, what d'you like particularly?

P₆: Fish and chips.

T: Yes. Anything else?

P$_6$: Um, apple and custard tart.

T: Yes. You're going to have fish and chips this week one day. Yes. Is there anything you don't like?

P$_6$: There's, er, to . . ., tomatoes – baked, or whatever they are. I can't remember what they're called. They're tomatoes – fried, I think.

T: You don't like those? Is it that you don't like tomatoes, or you don't like the way they're cooked?

P$_6$: I don't like tomatoes because they make me sick when I eat them. [. . .]

(T asks P$_6$ what sort of pet he would like, if any.)

P$_6$: We've got a pet cat at home, but we gave that to someone 'cause we moved house, and if we got it then that would go straight on to the road, 'cause that, that would go home, 'cause that doesn't know when we move. That doesn't know where to go.

T: Well that's very sensible, isn't it? Yes. If you had another pet would you choose another cat? Would you have another cat or would you want something else?

P$_6$: Um, a dog.

T: You'd like a dog, would you? Any special sort?

P$_6$: Probably a 'Dulux' dog.[5]

T: A 'Dulux'? Oh, d'you know what they really are, their proper name? They're an Old English Sheepdog. [. . .]

Pupil 7 (Boy, age 6;7)

[. . .]

T: Yesterday was Mothering Sunday. Did you do anything special?

P$_7$: Yes, we went to m. . . (indistinct), a church. I saw somebody being chr. . ., two people being christened.

T: Were they babies or grown-ups?

P$_7$: Babies.

T: Were they? Were they quiet?

P$_7$: The last one was being christened cried.

T: Yes. Did you enjoy it? Did you enjoy the service?

P$_7$: Yes.

T: Did you? Good.

P$_7$: They sang 'Sing Hosanna'.

T: Oh, you know that.

P$_7$: We sing it at school.

T: Yes, good. Um, had you made mummy a card or . . . ?

P$_7$: Yes, we made her a Mother's Day card and a Mother's Day present.

The Mother's Day present was a clay pot.

T: Good. Did you get it home safely?

P₇: Yes, we wrapped it up w. . ., in sellotape.

T: Yes. Was she pleased?

P₇: Yes.

T: Good. Stephen, what d'you, what d'you like doing most of all at school?

P₇: Work.

R: Ah, what sort of work?

P₇: Sums.

T: Would you tell us what sort of sums?

P₇: Hundreds, tens and units.⁶

R: Yes. How about writing and reading?

P₇: I like reading and I li. . ., I enjoy, enjoy writing.

T: What sort of books d'you like reading?

P₇: *Racing to Read.*⁷

T: What other, what story-books d'you like?

P₇: *Beago Scruff.*

T: Yes. When you pick your library books what sort of books d'you look for?

P₇: *Mr Men.*⁸

   [. . .]

T: I was wondering, Stephen. Have you got any pets at home?

P₇: We used to have a gerbil but it died with an infection.

T: Oh, can you . . . ?

P₇: It got poisonous, it got poisoned.

T: Oh dear!

P₇: It's in our garden, buried.

T: Yes, I don't know much about gerbils. Can you tell me something?

P₇: You've got to feed them about two a day, two . . . You've got to feed them . . . give them three, three meals, like us, a day.

T: What sort of thing d'you give them?

P₇: Don't really know.

   [. . .]

Pupil 8 (Girl, age 6;9)

   [. . .]

T: What d'you enjoy doing at school best of all?

P₈: Reading.

T: Um, would you tell us what sort of books you like?

P₈: Well, I like fairy-story books. I've got a Cinderella one at home and I've got 'Puss in Boots' and I've got 'Snow-White and the Seven Dwarfs'.

T: Yes. Have you read any of the books . . . (indistinct), of the fairy books that are called . . . – like *Orange Fairy Books*[9] . . . ?

P$_8$:   No.

T: . . . Or fairy stories, or *Blue Wide Range Books*?[10] Oh, you'll enjoy reading those when you're a bit older, I think. What d'you like doing best at week-ends?

P$_8$:   Playing with my cindies.

T: Dolls. Yes. What d'you do with them?

P$_8$:   I make them ride on the horse I've got and make them hold on to the reins, and they've got a car and go out camping.

T: Oh, you make up little adventures for them, do you?

P$_8$:   Yes.

    [. . .]

T: What d'you think of school lunches?

P$_8$:   Lovely.

T: You enjoy them, do you?

P$_8$:   Yes.

T: Have you a favourite amongst them?

P$_8$:   Doughnuts.

T: Doughnuts. Anything else favourite?

P$_8$:   Chips and beans and sausage.

T: Is there anything you don't enjoy?

P$_8$:   No.

T: Well, that's very good. At home, have you got any pets?

P$_8$:   I've got a cat called 'Panda'.

R: Ah, why's the cat called 'Panda'?

P$_8$:   Because she's black and white and she's got black spots and white spots on her.

R: Ah, how old is she?

P$_8$:   She's nearly four.

R: Ah, she's not, not young as far as cats go?

P$_8$:   No, she's twenty-eight in 'cat's age'.

    [. . .]

T: What d'you enjoy doing most of all with your friends in the playground?

P$_8$:   Playing 'Stuck-in-the-Mud'.

T: Oh, can you tell me how you play that?

P$_8$:   Well, one person pretends to be a witch and when they catch you, you have to put your arms out straight, and then if they're (?) . . . , and then the other person has to go under the arms — under one of the arms, and then that person who was holding their arms out can be free.

[. . .]

Pupil 9 (Girl, age 6;11)

[. . .]

T: Do you remember that picture on the wall there . . . (indistinct)?

P₉: Yes.

T: Can you tell us anything about it?

P₉: Well. (Pause: 8 seconds)

T: Who made it for me?

P₉: Daddy and Harry, daddy and my brother.

T: That's right. D'you know how they made it? Did you watch them?

P₉: Yes. My daddy got an old, um, pillow-case, um, I mean a pillow, and it was all feathers and then he glued it all to a bit of wood — painted.

T: Yes, what . . . ? Did Harry help him?

P₉: ?

T: Yes. Er, yesterday being Mothering Sunday, did you do anything special or . . . ?

P₉: Yes.

T: Would you tell us about it — what you did?

P₉: I asked mum what I could do and she said, er, 'Would you do the beds for me?' And I done mummy's, er, mine and daddy and Harry's bed.

[. . .]

T: What d'you like doing best of all at school, Frances?

P₉: Writing.

T: What sort of thing?

P₉: (Pause: 7 seconds)

T: What sort of thing d'you enjoy writing?

P₉: (Pause: 7 seconds)

T: Stories or . . . ?

P₉: Stories.

T: Yes.

R: Where d'you get the stories from? D'you make them up yourself or d'you get them from books? D'you . . . ?

P₉: (Interrupting R) I make them up.

R: You make them up. That's good.

T: What are your favourite games?

P₉: (Pause: 7 seconds) Playing on my bike.

T: You like playing on your bike, yes. What d'you like playing with your friends in the playground at school?

P₉: (Pause: 12 seconds)

T: At play-times, dinner times? What sort of thing d'you play with your friends?

P₉: 'Touchees'.

T: What sort of books d'you enjoy reading? — Because you read very nicely. What sort of books d'you like reading?

P₉: (Pause: 7 seconds)

T: Can you tell me?

P₉: Yes, fairy-tales and . . .

T: Yes. Have you a favourite?

P₉: Yes.

T: Will you tell us?

P₉: (Pause: 6 seconds)

T: Will you tell us what it is?

P₉: (Pause: 5 seconds)

R: Or is it a secret? Would you like to keep it to yourself?

P₉: (Nods)

      [. . .]

Discussion

The transcriptions do nothing to support the classical verbal deficit theory: none of the children interviewed could possibly be described as non-verbal, none is limited to monosyllabic utterances and there are no 'giant words', either! Without exception, in the course of a short interview, all the children produced at least one subordinate clause and at least one utterance consisting of a complete sentence. However, at first sight, the transcriptions may appear to lend some support to other, weaker versions of the deficit theory.

If one takes the transcriptions from each school collectively there is an overall difference in the kinds of answers given by the pupils at the two schools. In particular, there is a marked difference between the responses of Pupils 2 and 4 (School A) on the one hand, and those of Pupils 6, 7 and 8 (School B) on the other; more generally there was a greater tendency for pupils at School B to offer longer and fuller answers than their counterparts at School A. However, the differences are relative, not absolute. In the case of all the children (with the possible exception of Pupil 1), the majority of the pupils' utterances consisted of *yes*, *no*, a single word or short phrase or short sentence. Fuller answers — those which involved reasoning or which were in some sense descriptive — make up a minority of the responses in all cases, with the exception of Pupil 1. Nevertheless, a general, overall difference between the two sets of interviews remains and requires comment. Specifically, why were the pupils interviewed at School B more inclined to offer fuller answers?

From a formal point of view there are two types of questions: polar questions, which logically require *yes* or *no* as an answer, and *wh-*questions, which logically call for a different kind of answer. In formal terms, polar questions are closed, in the sense that they allow a choice between only two alternatives, while *wh-* questions are open in that they allow for a potentially unlimited range of replies. But this neat distinction holds only on a theoretical level, and in practice the situation is often very different. One may, for example, expand an answer to a polar question instead of replying merely with *yes* or *no*, and in certain circumstances apparently open questions are in fact closed. This latter situation occurs in particular where the questioner is willing to accept only one specific, preconceived answer and where at the same time an unequal power relationship between the questioner and the person expected to answer allows the former to insist on receiving a particular answer. As Barnes (1971) has illustrated in connection with the use of question-and-answer techniques in secondary school teaching this kind of situation is common in the classroom, and there is a tendency for teachers' questions to be closed, whatever the actual form in which they may be expressed. Commenting more generally on this phenomenon, Stubbs (1980, p. 115) notes:

It is clear from many studies of classroom language . . . that much of the spoken language in classrooms has no genuine communicative function. The majority of questions which teachers ask in many classrooms are not genuine questions asked because the teacher wants to know something: they are test questions, asked by a teacher who wants to know if a pupil knows something. It follows that a lot of the spoken language which pupils produce is monosyllabic, since they are simply responding to pseudo-questions. If children are to be encouraged to produce complex spoken language, they must be placed in social situations where they can initiate conversational exchanges and not just respond, and where the language has genuine communicative functions.

There are, of course, similarities between the classroom situation and research interviews, though the two types of situation are not identical. However, it is not surprising if children interpret questions asked in research interviews in much the same way as routine classroom questions.

In the transcriptions the pupils (except Pupil 1) show a strong tendency to interpret the great majority of questions as closed. What is remarkable in the transcriptions from School B is that the teacher managed in a number of instances to persuade the pupils that other interpretations of the questions were possible, and that there was no single, preconceived answer. It is interesting, however, that this re-interpretation was generally achieved only by means of a supplementary probe (such as 'Would you tell us about it?') after the children had treated the initial question as if it were closed. Whether the willingness of the pupils at School B to be persuaded that some of the questions were not closed can be accounted for solely by these supplementary probes, or whether it was also partly a matter of the style of teaching to which they were already accustomed, must remain a matter for speculation. It seems probable that other factors, including shyness, and the nature of some of the questions themselves also played a part. Another influence at work may be relative familiarity, or lack of it, in interacting with a wide range of adults. One cannot expect differences of this kind to disappear within the first two years of compulsory schooling – indeed, such differences can often be found among adults. It is noteworthy that, of the children interviewed, only Pupil 1 showed any indication of interpreting any part of the interview as a kind of completely open invitation to talk, and at one point in the transcription (when talking about 'Old Mother Hubbard' and in the following few lines) he seems to be briefly indifferent to the teacher's questions and continues to say what he wants to say. But in general, all the pupils showed a very high degree of awareness of the social conventions of the interview, despite the fact that some were initially rather shy.

The fact that differences of interactional range and experience often have linguistic correlates does not justify a theory of codes. Nor does it call for a complex taxonomy of different types of language used for different purposes, as proposed by Tough (1976, pp. 78–80), who establishes 37 different categories of language-use. One of the greatest weaknesses of her approach is that it tends to focus on linguistic indicators of interaction rather than on interaction itself, and — most serious of all — the central role of the teacher in classroom interaction tends to escape adequate notice.

If children are unwilling or apparently unable to talk freely and naturally to teachers the purely linguistic aspect of the matter is among the least of the real problems involved; and there is a danger that by focusing on language-use other, more fundamental problems may be overlooked. In short, verbal deficit theories place far too great a burden of explanation on language, with the inevitable mystification that this involves. Nowhere is this epitomised more clearly than in the slogan, quoted with approval by Doughty and Thornton (1973, p. 5), that 'Educational failure is primarily *linguistic* failure'. It would be better to admit that differences in pupils' responses in interviews and in the classroom are influenced by many different factors and that no simple explanation is possible.

Notes

1. Admittedly, two ninety-minute visits of this kind are probably insufficient.
2. See Stubbs (1976a, pp. 31–2).
3. *Fletcher* refers to the basic mathematics course-materials in use in the school, and is used by some of the children (and teachers) to denote the actual subject as well.
4. *Seven* refers to Book 7A in the *Ladybird Series; Old Dog Tom* to a book in the *Beacon Series*.
5. 'Dulux' paints had recently been advertised on commercial television, and an Old English Sheepdog had been used in the advertisement.
6. 'Hundreds, tens, units' refers in this context to addition and subtraction up to 999.
7. This refers to a basic reader in use in the school.
8. This refers to a series of story-books in use in the school.
9. As note 8.
10. As note 7.

BIBLIOGRAPHY

I. United Kingdom Official Publications (Arranged by Departments of State, etc.)

Notes

1. Acts of Parliament are not included in this bibliography.
2. All the items in this section were published by HMSO, London, unless otherwise indicated.

Prime Minister

1963–4   *Higher Education: Report of the Committee Appointed by the Prime Minister under the Chairmanship of Lord Robbins 1961–63*, 1963, Cmnd 2154
          Appendix I: *The Demand for Places in Higher Education*, 1963, Cmnd 2154-I
          Appendix II: *Students and Their Education* (2 vols), 1964, Cmnd 2154-II-I and 2154-II-II
          Appendix III: *Teachers in Higher Education*, 1963, Cmnd 2154-III
          Appendix IV: *Administrative, Financial and Economic Aspects of Higher Education*, 1963, Cmnd 2154-IV
          Appendix V: *Higher Education in Other Countries*, 1964, Cmnd 2154-V
          ('Robbins Report, 1963')

Privy Council

   Committee of Council on Education (1839–56)
1846–56   HMIs' Reports
   Education Department (1856–99)
1857–99   HMIs' Reports

Board of Education (1899–1944)

1920   *Report of the Departmental Committee on Scholarships and Free Places*, Cmd 968
1921   *The Teaching of English in England, Being the Report of the Departmental Committee Appointed by the President of the Board of Education to Inquire into the Position of English in the Educational System of England* ('Newbolt

Report, 1921')

1924   *Report of the Consultative Committee on Psychological Tests of Educable Capacity and Their Possible Use in the Public System of Education*

1926   *Report of the Consultative Committee on the Education of the Adolescent* ('Hadow Report, 1926')

1931   *Report of the Consultative Committee on the Primary School* ('Hadow Report, 1931')

1933   *Report of the Consultative Committee on Infant and Nursery Schools* ('Hadow Report, 1933')

1938   *Report of the Consultative Committee on Secondary Education with Special Reference to Grammar Schools and Technical High Schools* ('Spens Report, 1938')

1943   *Curriculum and Examinations in Secondary Schools: Report of the Committee of the Secondary School Examinations Council Appointed by the President of the Board of Education in 1941* ('Norwood Report, 1943')
         Educational Reconstruction, Cmd 6458

         Handbook . . . First published in 1905 under the title *Suggestions for the Consideration of Teachers and Others Concerned in the Work of Public Elementary Schools*, Cd 2638. 2nd ed., 1912, 3rd ed., 1914, 4th ed., 1918, 5th ed., 1923, 6th ed., re-titled *Handbook of Suggestions for the Consideration of Teachers and Others Concerned in the Work of Public Elementary Schools*, 1927, 7th ed., 1937

Ministry of Education (1944–64)

1947   *The New Secondary Education* (Ministry of Education Pamphlet No. 9)

1954   *Early Leaving: A Report of the Central Advisory Council for Education (England)*
         Language: Some Suggestions for Teachers of English and Others in Primary and Secondary Schools and in Further Education (Ministry of Education Pamphlet No. 26)

1959   *Primary Education: Suggestions for the Consideration of Teachers and Others Concerned with the Work of Primary Schools*

1959–60 *15 to 18: A Report of the Central Advisory Council for Education (England)*, Vol. 1: *Report*, 1959; Vol. 2:

Surveys, 1960 ('Crowther Report, 1959')

1963   *Half Our Future: A Report of the Central Advisory Council for Education (England)* ('Newsom Report, 1963')

Department of Education and Science (1964 and later)

1967   *Children and Their Primary Schools: A Report of the Central Advisory Council for Education (England)*, Vol. 1: *The Report*; Vol. 2: *Appendices* ('Plowden Report, 1967')

1975   *A Language for Life: Report of the Committee of Inquiry Appointed by the Secretary of State for Education and Science under the Chairmanship of Sir Alan Bullock F.B.A.* ('Bullock Report, 1975')

1977   *Educating Our Children: Four Subjects for Debate. A Background Paper for the Regional Conferences, February and March 1977*
          Education in Schools: A Consultative Document, Cmnd 6869

Scottish Office (Scottish Education Department)

1947   *Secondary Education: A Report of the Advisory Council on Education in Scotland*, HMSO, Edinburgh, Cmd 7005

II. Books and Articles

Adams, (Sir) J. (1897) *The Herbartian Psychology Applied to Education, Being a Series of Essays Applying the Psychology of Johann Friedrich Herbart*, Isbister, London
—— (1912) *The Evolution of Educational Theory*, Macmillan, London
—— (1928) *Modern Developments in Educational Practice,* 2nd ed., University of London Press, London (1st ed. published in 1922)
Adlam, D.S., with the assistance of Turner, G. and Lineker, L. (1977) *Code in Context*, Routledge and Kegan Paul, London
Anon. (1872) *Handbook on the Teaching and Management of Elementary Schools. By the Editor of the 'National Schoolmaster'*, John Heywood, Manchester
Bagley, W.C. (1925) *Determinism in Education: A Series of Papers on the Relative Influence of Inherited and Acquired Traits in Determining Intelligence, Achievement, and Character*, Warwick and York, Baltimore

Bailey, B.L. (1965) 'Toward a New Perspective in Negro English
   Dialectology', *American Speech*, **40**, 171–77
Bain, A. (1879) *Education as a Science*, 3rd ed., C. Kegan Paul, London
   (1st ed. published in 1879)
Ballard, P.B. (1920) *Mental Tests*, Hodder and Stoughton, London
—— (1922) *Group Tests of Intelligence*, Hodder and Stoughton,
   London
—— (1923) *The New Examiner*, Hodder and Stoughton, London
Banks, O. (1971) *The Sociology of Education*, 2nd ed., B.T. Batsford,
   London (1st ed. published in 1968)
Baratz, J.C. (1969) 'A Bi-Dialectal Task for Determining Language
   Proficiency in Economically Disadvantaged Negro Children', *Child
   Development*, **40**, 889–901
—— (1970a) 'Teaching Reading in an Urban Negro School System',
   in Williams (ed., 1970), 11–24
—— (1970b) 'Educational Considerations for Teaching Standard
   English to Negro Children', in Fasold and Shuy (eds., 1970), 20–40
—— and Baratz, S.S. (1970) 'Early Childhood Intervention: The
   Social Science Base of Institutional Racism', *Harvard Educational
   Review*, **40**, 29–50
—— and Shuy, R.W. (eds., 1969), *Teaching Black Children to Read*,
   Center for Applied Linguistics, Washington, D.C. (*Urban Language
   Series*, **4**)
Barlow, M. and Macan, H. (1903) *The Education Act, 1902, With
   Notes, Together with a Summary of the Existing Law and of the
   Provisions of the Education Act, 1902 . . .* , 2nd ed., Butterworth,
   London (1st ed. published in 1903)
Barnes, D. (1973) *Language in the Classroom*, Open University Press,
   Bletchley, Buckinghamshire (Open University Course E262, Block 4)
—— *et al.* (1971) *Language, the Learner and the School: A Research
   Report by Douglas Barnes with a Contribution by James Britton
   and a Discussion Document prepared by Harold Rosen on Behalf of
   the London Association for the Teaching of English*, revised ed.,
   Penguin Books, Harmondsworth, Middlesex (1st ed. published in
   1969)
Barnett, P.A. (1899) *Common Sense in Education and Teaching: An
   Introduction to Practice*, Longmans, London
Bartley, (Sir) G.C.T. (1871) *The Schools for the People, Containing
   the History, Development, and Present Working of Each Description
   of English School for the Industrial and Poorer Classes*, Bell and
   Daldy, London

Belcourt, S. and Gordon, J.C.B. (1980) 'A Classroom Confrontation', *English in Education*, **14**, Pt 1, 10–15

Benson, A.C. (1902) *The Schoolmaster: A Commentary upon the Aims and Methods of an Assistant-Master in a Public School*, John Murray, London

Bereiter, C. and Engelmann, S. (1966) *Teaching Disadvantaged Children in the Preschool*, Prentice-Hall, Englewood Cliffs, New Jersey

—— , Engelmann, S., Osborn, J. and Reidford, P.A. (1966) 'An Academically Oriented Pre-School for Culturally Deprived Children', in Hechinger, F.M. (ed.), *Preschool Education Today: New Approaches to Teaching Three-, Four-, and Five-Year-Olds*, Doubleday, Garden City, New York, pp. 105–35

Bernstein, B. (1958) 'Some Sociological Determinants of Perception', in Bernstein (1971/74), pp. 23–41

—— (1959) 'A Public Language: Some Sociological Implications of a Linguistic Form', in Bernstein (1971/74), pp. 42–60

—— (1960) 'Language and Social Class', in Bernstein (1971/74), pp. 61–67

—— (1961a) 'Social Class and Linguistic Development', in Halsey, A.H., Floud, J. and Anderson, C.A. (eds.), *Education, Economy and Society: A Reader in the Sociology of Education*, Collier-Macmillan, London, pp. 288–314

—— (1961b) 'Social Structure, Language and Learning', in De Cecco, J.P. (ed.), *The Psychology of Language, Thought and Instruction: Readings*, Holt, Rinehart and Winston, New York, pp. 89–103

—— (1962a) 'Linguistic Codes, Hesitation Phenomena and Intelligence', in Bernstein (1971/74), pp. 76–94

—— (1962b) 'Social Class, Linguistic Codes and Grammatical Elements', in Bernstein (1971/74), pp. 95–117

—— (1964) 'Elaborated and Restricted Codes: Their Social Origins and Some Consequences', in Gumperz, J.J. and Hymes, D. (eds.), *The Ethnography of Communication (Monograph Issue of American Anthropologist*, **66**, No. 6, Pt 2, 55–69)

—— (1965) 'A Socio-Linguistic Approach to Social Learning', in Bernstein (1971/74), pp. 118–39

—— (1967) 'The Role of Speech in the Development and Transmission of Culture', in Klopf, G.J. and Hohman, W.A. (eds.), *Perspectives on Learning*, published for the Bank Street College of Education by The Mental Health Materials Center, Inc., New York, pp. 15–45

Bernstein, B. (1969) 'A Critique of the Concept of Compensatory Education', in Bernstein (1971/74), pp. 190–201

—— (1970) 'A Socio-Linguistic Approach to Socialization: With Some Reference to Educability', in Bernstein (1971/74), pp. 143–69

—— (1971a) 'Social Class, Language and Socialization', in Bernstein (1971/74), pp. 170–89

—— (1971b) Introduction to Bernstein (1971/74), pp. 1–20

—— (1971/74) *Class, Codes and Control, Vol. 1: Theoretical Studies towards a Sociology of Language*, Routledge and Kegan Paul, London (1st ed., 1971, 2nd revised ed., 1974. The 2nd ed. contains an Addendum and Postscript which are not in the 1st ed.)

—— (1973) Postscript to Bernstein (1971/74), in 2nd ed. only, pp. 237–57

—— (ed., 1973) *Class, Codes and Control, Vol. 2: Applied Studies towards a Sociology of Education*, Routledge and Kegan Paul, London

Birchenough, C. (1938) *History of Elementary Education in England and Wales from 1800 to the Present Day*, 3rd ed., University Tutorial Press, London (1st ed. published in 1914)

Black Paper 1 [1969] Cox, C.B. and Dyson, A.E. (eds.), *Fight for Education: A Black Paper*, Critical Quarterly Society, London, n.d.

Black Paper 2 [1969] Cox, C.B. and Dyson, A.E. (eds.), *The Crisis in Education: Black Paper 2*, Critical Quarterly Society, London, n.d.

Blakiston, J.R. (1879) *The Teacher: Hints on School Management*, Macmillan, London

Block, N.J. and Dworkin, G. (eds., 1976) *The IQ Controversy: Critical Readings*, Pantheon Books, New York

Boydell, D. (1975) 'Systematic Observation in Informal Classrooms', in Chanan and Delamont (eds., 1975), pp. 183–97

Bray, S.E. (1914) *School Organisation, with an Introduction by Sir James Yoxall*, 3nd ed., University Tutorial Press, London (1st ed. published in 1905)

Bullock Report (1975) – See Official Publications

Burling, R. (1970) *Man's Many Voices: Language in Its Cultural Context*, Holt, Rinehart and Winston, New York

Burt, (Sir) C. (1921) *Mental and Scholastic Tests*, P.S. King, London

—— (1923) *Handbook of Tests for Use in Schools*, P.S. King, London

—— (1943a) 'Ability and Income', *British Journal of Educational Psychology*, **13**, 83–98

—— (1943b) 'The Education of the Young Adolescent: The

Psychological Implications of the Norwood Report', *British Journal of Educational Psychology*, **13**, 126–40

Calderwood, H. (1875) *On Teaching: Its Ends and Means*, 2nd ed., Edmonton and Douglas, Edinburgh (1st ed. published in 1874)

Carroll, J.B. (1956) Introduction to Carroll (ed., 1956), pp. 1–34

—— (ed., 1956) *Language, Thought and Reality: Selected Writings of Benjamin Lee Whorf, edited and with an Introduction by John B. Carroll. Foreword by Stuart Chase*, MIT Press, Cambridge, Mass.

—— (1964) *Language and Thought*, Prentice-Hall, Englewood Cliffs, New Jersey

Cassidy, F.G. (1968) 'Tracing the Pidgin Element in Jamaican Creole (with Notes on Method and the Nature of Pidgin Vocabularies)', in Hymes, D. (ed.) *Pidginization and Creolization of Languages: Proceedings of a Conference Held at the University of the West Indies, Mona, Jamaica, April 1968*, CUP, London, 1971, pp. 203–21

Cazden, C.B. (1970) 'The Neglected Situation in Child Language Research and Education', in Williams (ed., 1970), pp. 81–101

Chanan, G. and Delamont, S. (eds., 1975) *Frontiers of Classroom Research*, National Foundation for Educational Research Publishing Co., Windsor, Berkshire

—— and Gilchrist, L. (1974) *What School Is For*, Methuen, London

Chomsky, N. (1979) *Language and Responsibility, Based on Conversations with Mitsou Ronat*. Translated from the French by J. Viertel, Harvester Press, Hassocks, Sussex

Clarke, A.M. and Clarke, A.D.B. (1976) 'The Formative Years?' in Clarke and Clarke (eds., 1976), pp. 3–24

—— (eds., 1976) *Early Experience: Myth and Evidence*, Open Books, London

Clarke, (Sir) F. (1940) *Education and Social Change: An English Interpretation*, Sheldon Press, London

—— (1941) 'The Social Function of Secondary Education', *Sociological Review*, OS **33**, 105–25

Collar, G. and Crook, C.W. (1900) *School Management and Methods of Instruction with Special Reference to Schools*, Macmillan, London

Collins, G. [1887] *Notes on School Management*, Moffat and Paige, London, n.d. (1st ed. published in 1884)

Collins, R.N. (1843) *The Teacher's Companion: Designed to Exhibit the Principles of Sunday School Instruction and Discipline*, 2nd ed., Houlston and Stoneman, London (1st ed. published in 1842)

Cook-Gumperz, J. (1973) *Social Control and Socialization: A Study of Class Differences in the Language of Maternal Control*, Routledge and Kegan Paul, London

Coulthard, M. (1969) 'A Discussion of Restricted and Elaborated Codes', *Educational Review*, 22, 38–50

Coupland, W.C. (1889) *The Elements of Mental and Moral Science as Applied to Teaching*, Joseph Hughes, London

Cowham, J.H. (1895) *A New School Method (Complete) for Pupil Teachers and Students*, 2nd ed., Simpkin, Marshall, Hamilton, Kent and Co., London (1st ed. published in 1894)

—— (1896) *The Principles of Oral Teaching and Mental Training: An Introduction to the Elements of Psychology and Ethics . . .* , 5th (?) ed., Simpkin, Marshall, Hamilton, Kent and Co., London (1st ed. published in 1890)

Cox, T.A. and Macdonald, R.F. (1897) *The Suggestive Handbook of Practical School Method: A Guide to the School-Room and the Examination Room*, 2nd ed., Blackie, London (1st ed. published in 1896)

Creber, J.W.P. (1972) *Lost for Words: Language and Educational Failure*, Penguin Books in association with the National Association for the Teaching of English, Harmondsworth, Middlesex

Crowther Report (1959) – See Official Publications

Currie, J. [1878] *The Principles and Practice of Common-School Education*, 2nd ed., Thomas Laurie, Edinburgh, n.d. (1st ed. published in 1861)

Curtis, S.J. (1952) *Education in Britain since 1900*, Andrew Dakers, London

—— and Boultwood, M.E.A. (1964) *An Introductory History of English Education since 1800*, 3rd ed., University Tutorial Press, London (1st ed. published in 1960)

Dale, P.S. (1976) *Language Development: Structure and Function*, 2nd ed., Holt, Rinehart and Winston, New York (1st ed. published in 1972)

Delamont, S. (1976) *Interaction in the Classroom*, Methuen, London

Dent, H.C. (1949) *Secondary Education for All: Origins and Development in England*, Routledge and Kegan Paul, London

Deutsch, M. *et al.* (1967) *The Disadvantaged Child: Selected Papers of Martin Deutsch and Associates*, Basic Books, New York

Dillard, J.L. (1968) 'Nonstandard Negro Dialects: Convergence or Divergence?', *Florida FL Reporter*, 6, Pt 2, 9–12

—— (1972) *Black English: Its History and Use in the United States*,

Random House, New York

Dittmar, N. (1976) *Sociolinguistics: A Critical Survey of Theory and Application*. Translated from the German by P. Sand, P.A.M. Seuren and K. Whiteley, Edward Arnold, London

Dodd, C.I. (1898) *Introduction to the Herbartian Principles of Teaching*, Swan Sonnenschein, London

—— (1906) *The Child and the Curriculum*, Swan Sonnenschein, London

Doughty, P. and Thornton, G. (1973) *Language Study, the Teacher and the Learner*, Edward Arnold, London

Douglas, J.W.B. (1964) *The Home and the School: A Study of Ability and Attainment in the Primary School*, MacGibbon and Kee, London

Dumville, B. (1913) *Child Mind: An Introduction to Psychology for Teachers*, University Tutorial Press, London

Dunn, H. (1837) *Popular Education; Or, The Normal School Manual: Containing Practical Suggestions for Daily and Sunday School Teachers, in a Series of Letters*, Sunday School Union, London

Edwards, J.R. (1979) *Language and Disadvantage*, Edward Arnold, London

Eysenck, H.J. (1962) *Know Your Own I.Q.*, Penguin Books, Harmondsworth, Middlesex

—— (1971) *Race, Intelligence and Education*, Temple Smith, London

—— (1973) *The Inequality of Man*, Temple Smith, London

Fasold, R. and Shuy, R.W. (1970) Introduction to Fasold and Shuy (eds., 1970), pp. ix–xvi

—— (eds., 1970) *Teaching Standard English in the Inner City*, Center for Applied Linguistics, Washington, DC (*Urban Language Series*, 6)

Ferguson, C.A. (1959) 'Diglossia', *Word*, 15, 325–40

Findlay, J.J. (1902) *Principles of Class Teaching*, Macmillan, London

—— [1912] *The School: An Introduction to the Study of Education*, Williams and Norgate, London, n.d.

Fitch, (Sir) J.G. (1881) *Lectures on Teaching Delivered in the University of Cambridge during the Lent Term, 1880*, University Press, Cambridge

Fleming, C.M. (1944) *The Social Psychology of Education: An Introduction and Guide to Its Study*, Kegan Paul, Trench, Trubner and Co., London

—— (1947) 'Guidance at the Secondary Stage', *The Schoolmaster and Woman Teacher's Chronicle*, 28 August 1947, pp. 170–1

Fleming, C.M. (1948) *Adolescence. Its Social Psychology: with an Introduction to Recent Findings from the Fields of Anthropology, Physiology, Medicine, Psychometrics and Sociometry*, Routledge and Kegan Paul, London

Floud, J.E. (ed.), Halsey, A.H. and Martin, F.M. (1957) *Social Class and Educational Opportunity*, William Heinemann, London

Flude, M. (1974) 'Sociological Accounts of Differential Educational Attainment', in Flude, M. and Ahier, J. (eds.) *Educability, Schools and Ideology*, Croom Helm, London, pp. 15–52

Ford, D. (1955) *The Deprived Child and the Community*, Constable, London

Francis, H. (1977) *Language in Teaching and Learning*, George Allen and Unwin, London

Freeman, P. (1973) 'The Study of French Society in CSE Mode III Courses', in *Modern Languages and European Studies: Papers from a Conference . . .*, Centre for Information on Language Teaching and Research (CILT), London (*CILT Reports and Papers*, 9)

Gahagan, D.M. and Gahagan, G.A. (1970) *Talk Reform: Explorations in Language for Infant School Children*, Routledge and Kegan Paul, London

Galton, (Sir) F. (1865) 'Hereditary Talent and Character', *Macmillan's Magazine*, 12, 157–66 and 319–27

—— (1869) *Hereditary Genius: An Inquiry into Its Laws and Consequences*, Macmillan, London

—— (1883) *Inquiries into Human Faculty and Its Development*, Macmillan, London

—— and Schuster, E. (1906) *Noteworthy Families (Modern Science): An Index to Kinships in Near Degrees between Persons Whose Achievements Are Honourable, And Have Been Publicly Recorded*, John Murray, London. (*Publications of the Eugenics Record Office of the University of London*, 1)

Garlick, A.H. (1907) *A New Manual of Method*, 7th ed., Longmans, London (1st ed. published in 1896)

Giles, H. (1971) 'Our Reactions to Accent', *New Society*, 14 October 1971, pp. 713–15

—— and Powesland, P.F. (1975) *Speech Style and Social Evaluation*, Academic Press in Co-operation with the European Association of Experimental Social Psychology, London

Gill, J. (1883) *Introductory Text Book to School Education, Method and School Management: A Treatise on the Principles, Aims and*

Instruments of Primary Education, new ed., London. (1st ed. published *c*. 1856)

Ginsburg, H. (1972) *The Myth of the Deprived Child: Poor Children's Intellect and Education*, Prentice-Hall, Englewood Cliffs, New Jersey

Glass, D.V. (ed., 1954) *Social Mobility in Britain*, Routledge and Kegan Paul, London

Gordon, J.C.B. (1976a) 'An Examination of Bernstein's Theory of Restricted and Elaborated Codes', *UEA Papers in Linguistics*, 2, 1–21

—— (1976b) 'Concepts of Verbal Deficit in Bernstein's Writings on Language and Social Class', *Nottingham Linguistic Circular*, 5, No. 2, 31–8

—— (1977) 'Linguistics and the Concept of Verbal Deficit', *Nottingham Linguistic Circular*, 6, No. 2, 51–9

—— (1978a) 'Folk-Linguistics and the Essence of Verbal Deficit Theories', *UEA Papers in Linguistics*, 7, 11–20

—— (1978b) 'The Reception of Bernstein's Sociolinguistic Theory among Primary School Teachers, Norwich 1978 (*UEA Papers in Linguistics, Supplement No. 1*)

Gray, J.L. and Moshinsky, P. (1935a) 'Ability and Opportunity in English Education', *Sociological Review*, OS 27, 113–62

—— (1935b) 'Ability and Educational Opportunity in Relation to Parental Occupation', *Sociological Review*, OS 27, 281–327

Gunn, J. (1895) *Class Teaching and Management*, Nelson, London

—— (1906) *The Infant School: Its Principles and Methods*, Nelson, London

Hackwood, F.W. (1897) *The Practical Method of Class Management: A Ready Guide of Useful Hints to Young Class Teachers*, 2nd ed., George Philip, London (1st ed. published in 1896)

Hadow Report (1926)
—— Report (1931) — See Official Publications
—— Report (1933)

Halliday, M.A.K. (1975) *Learning How to Mean: Explorations in the Development of Language*, Edward Arnold, London

——, McIntosh, A. and Strevens, P. (1964) *The Linguistic Sciences and Language Teaching*, Longmans, London

Harding, F.E. (1877) *Practical Handbook of School-Management and Teaching for Teachers, Pupil Teachers, and Students*, new ed., Thomas Laurie, Edinburgh (1st ed. published in 1872)

Hawkins, P.R. (1969) 'Social Class, the Nominal Group and Reference', in Bernstein (ed., 1973), pp. 81—92

Hawkins, P.R. (1973) 'The Influence of Sex, Social Class and Pause-Location in the Hesitation Phenomena of Seven-Year-Old Children', in Bernstein (ed., 1973), pp. 235—50

—— (1977) *Social Class, the Nominal Group and Verbal Strategies*, Routledge and Kegan Paul, London

Hayward, F.H. (1908) *Education and the Heredity Spectre*, Watts, London

—— (1912) *Educational Administration and Criticism*, Ralph, Holland and Co., London

Henderson, A. [1904] *Some Notes on Teaching*, Arthur Shimeld, Nottingham, n.d.

Herriot, P. (1971) *Language and Teaching: A Psychological View*, Methuen, London

Herrnstein, R.J. (1973) *IQ in the Meritocracy*, Allen Lane, London (1st ed. published in the USA, 1973)

Hogben, L. (1933) *Nature and Nurture, being the William Withering Memorial Lectures . . . for the Year 1933*, Williams and Norgate, London

—— (1938) Introduction to Part II of Hogben, L. (ed.), *Political Arithmetic: A Symposium of Population Studies*, George Allen and Unwin, London, pp. 331—3

Hoggart, R. (1957) *The Uses of Literacy: Aspects of Working Class Life with Special Reference to Publications and Entertainments*, Chatto and Windus, London

Holmes, E. [G.A.] (1911) *What Is and What Might Be: A Study of Education in General and Elementary Education in Particular*, Constable, London

Hornsey, A.W. (1972) 'A Foreign Language for All?', in Perren, G.E. (ed.), *Teaching Modern Languages across the Ability Range: Papers from a Conference . . .*, Centre for Information on Language Teaching and Research (CILT), London (*CILT Reports and Papers*, 8), pp. 32—6

Houston, S.H. (1969) 'A Sociolinguistic Consideration of the Black English of Children in Northern Florida', *Language*, 45, No. 3, 599—607

—— (1971) 'A Re-Examination of Some Assumptions about the Language of the Disadvantaged Child', in Chess, S. and Thomas, A. (eds.), *Annual Progress in Child Psychiatry and Child Development 1971*, Butterworth, London, 1972

Hughes, R.E. (1905) *School Training*, University Tutorial Press, London

Hunt, J. McV. (1961) *Intelligence and Experience*, Ronald Press, New York

Hurt, J. (1972) *Education in Evolution: Church, State, Society and Popular Education 1800–1870*, Paladin, London (1st ed. published in 1971)

Hymes, D. (1970) 'Bilingual Education: Linguistic vs. Sociolinguistic Bases', in Alatis, J.E. (ed.), *Report of the Twenty-First Round Table Meeting on Linguistics and Language Studies*, Georgetown University Press, Washington, DC, pp. 69–76

Ingham, C.B. (1903) *Education in Accordance with Natural Law: Suggestions for the Consideration of Parents, Teachers, and Social Reformers*, Novello, London

Isaacs, S. (1932a) *The Nursery Years: The Mind of the Child from Birth to Six Years*, 2nd ed., George Routledge, London (1st ed. published in 1929)

—— (1932b) *The Children We Teach: Seven to Eleven Years*, University of London Press, London

Jackson, L.A. (1974) 'The Myth of Elaborated and Restricted Code', *Higher Education Review*, **6**, Pt 2, 65–81

James, C.V. and Rouve, S. (1973) *Survey of Curricula and Performance in Modern Languages 1971–72*, Centre for Educational Technology, University of Sussex, and Centre for Information on Language Teaching and Research, London

Jencks, C., Smith, M., Acland, H., Bane, M.J., Cohen, D., Gintis, H., Heyns, B. and Michelson, S. (1972) *Inequality: A Reassessment of the Effect of Family and Schooling in America*, Basic Books, New York

Jensen, A.R. (1968) 'Social Class and Verbal Learning', in Deutsch, M., Katz, I. and Jensen, A.R. (eds.), *Social Class, Race and Psychological Development*, Holt, Rinehart and Winston, New York

—— (1969) 'How Much Can We Boost IQ and Scholastic Achievement?', *Harvard Educational Review*, **39**, 1–123

Jolly, W. (1874) *The Public School, Its Organization, Management and Teaching: Being Suggestions to School Boards Bearing on the Efficiency of Common Schools, in Addresses Delivered, in March, at Elgin, Forres, Inverness and Nairn*, published by request, Thomas Laurie, Edinburgh

Jordan, D. (1943) 'Ability and Opportunity in Education', in Woodhead, E.W. (ed.), *Education Handbook*, Jarrold, Norwich, pp. 47–58

Kay, D. (1883) *Education and Educators*, Kegan Paul, Trench and Co., London

Keddie, N. (1972) 'Cultural Deprivation: A Case in Point' (*Social Differentiation II*), in *Sorting Them Out: Two Essays on Social Differentiation*, Open University Press, Milton Keynes, Buckinghamshire (Course E282, Units 9 and 10)

Kennedy-Fraser, D. (1923) *The Psychology of Education*, Methuen, London

King, R.A. (1969) *Education*, Longmans, London

Kingsley, C. (1874) *Health and Education*, Daldy, Isbister and Co., London

Klein, J. (1972) Review of 1st ed. of Bernstein 1971/74, *British Journal of Educational Studies*, 20, 236–7

Labov, W. (1969) 'The Logic of Non-Standard English', in Alatis, J.E. (ed.), *Report of the Twentieth Round Table Meeting on Linguistics and Language Studies*, Georgetown University Press, Washington, DC, 1970 (*Georgetown Monograph Series on Languages and Linguistics*, 22, 1–39

—— (1972) *Language in the Inner City: Studies in the Black English Vernacular*, Pennsylvania University Press, Philadelphia

——, Cohen, P., Robins, C. and Lewis, J., *A Study of the Non-standard English of Negro and Puerto Rican Speakers in New York City*, 2 vols., Final Report, US Office of Education Co-operative Research Project No. 3288, Columbia University, New York

Landon, J. (1894) *The Principles and Practice of Teaching and Class Management*, Alfred M. Holden, London

Laurie, S.S. (1867) *On Primary Instruction in Relation to Education*, William Blackwood, Edinburgh

—— (1892) *Institutes of Education Comprising an Introduction to Rational Psychology, Designed (Partly) as a Text-Book for Universities and Colleges*, James Thin, Edinburgh

Lawton, D. (1968) *Social Class, Language and Education*, Routledge and Kegan Paul, London

Lazar, I. and Darlington, R. (1978) *Lasting Effects after Preschool: A Report by the Central Staff of the Consortium for Longitudinal Studies (formerly the Consortium on Developmental Continuity)*, US Department of Health, Education and Welfare, DHEW Publication No. (OHDS)79-30178, Washington DC

Lee, V. (1973) *Social Relationships and Language: Some Aspects of the Work of Basil Bernstein with an Account of the Theory of Codes by Basil Bernstein*, Open University Press, Bletchley, Buckinghamshire (Course E262, Block 3)

Levitas, M. (1976) 'A Culture of Deprivation', *Marxism Today*, 20,

108–15

Lindsay, K. (1926) *Social Progress and Educational Waste, Being a Study of the 'Free-Place' and Scholarships System*, George Routledge, London

Little, A. and Smith, G. (1971) *Strategies of Compensation: A Review of Educational Projects for the Disadvantaged in the United States*, Centre for Educational Research and Innovation (CERI), OECD, Paris

Lodge, K.R. (1977) 'A Note on Personal Reference in Colloquial English', *UEA Papers in Linguistics*, 4, 38–45

Lodge, (Sir) O. (1905) *School Teaching and School Reform: A Course of Four Lectures on School Curricula and Methods, Delivered to Secondary Teachers and Teachers in Training at Birmingham during February 1905*, Williams and Norgate, London

Lowndes, G.A.N. (1969) *The Silent Social Revolution: An Account of the Expansion of Public Education in England and Wales 1895–1965*, 2nd ed., OUP, London (1st ed. published in 1937)

Luria, A.R. and Yudovich, F.Ia. (1959) *Speech and the Development of Mental Processes in the Child: An Experimental Investigation . . .*, edited by Joan Simon [Translated by O. Kovasc and J. Simon], Staples Press, London (Original version first published in Russian in 1956)

Macaulay, R.K.S. (1977) with the assistance of Trevelyan, G.D., *Language, Social Class and Education: A Glasgow Study*, Edinburgh University Press, Edinburgh

McPherson, A. (1949) 'The Philosophical Aspects of Intelligence', *Modern Quarterly*, NS 4, 218–37

Mason, C.M. (1905) *School Education*, Kegan Paul, Trench, Trübner and Co., London (*Home Education*, 3)

Mark, [H.] T. [1913] *Modern Views on Education*, Collins, London, n.d.

Markby, T. (1868) *Practical Essays on Education*, Strachan, London

Medlicott, P. (1975) 'Language and Class', *New Society*, 5 June 1975, pp. 575–6

Morris, M. (1951) 'Intelligence Testing and the Class System of Education', *Modern Quarterly*, NS 6, Pt 2, 163–77

Musgrove, F. (1966) *The Family, Education and Society*, Routledge and Kegan Paul, London

National Society (1880) *An Advanced Manual of Teaching for Teachers of Elementary and Higher Schools, Specially Adapted to the New Code*, National Society's Depository, London

Newbolt Report (1921) – See Official Publications
Newsom Report (1963) – See Official Publications
Nisbet, J.D. (1953) *Family Environment: A Direct Effect of Family Size on Intelligence*, Eugenics Society and Cassell, *Occasional Papers on Eugenics*, 8
Norwood Report (1943) – See Official Publications
Nunn, (Sir) [T.] P. (1945) *Education: Its Data and First Principles*, 3rd ed., Edward Arnold, London (1st ed. published in 1920)
Oevermann, U. (1972) *Sprache und soziale Herkunft: Ein Beitrag zur Analyse schichtenspezifischer Sozialisationsprozesse und ihrer Bedeutung für den Schulerfolg*, Suhrkamp Verlag, Frankfurt am Main
O'Neil, W.A. (1968) 'Paul Roberts' Rules of Order: The Misuses of Linguistics in the Classroom', *Urban Review*, 2, Pt 7, 12–16
Plowden Report (1967) – See Official Publications
Pritchard, D.G. (1963) *Education and the Handicapped 1760–1960*, Routledge and Kegan Paul, London
Rahtz, F.J. (1909) *Higher English*, 4th ed., Methuen, London (1st ed. published in 1907)
Raymont, T. (1904) *The Principles of Education*, Longmans, London
Richmond, W.K. (1945) *Education in England*, Penguin Books, Harmondsworth, Middlesex
Riessmann, F. (1962) *The Culturally Deprived Child*, Harper and Row, New York
Robbins Report (1963) – See Official Publications
Roberts, G.R. (1972) *English in Primary Schools*, Routledge and Kegan Paul, London
Robins, S. (1850) *The Church Schoolmaster*, Francis and John Rivington, London
Robinson, R. (1869) *Teacher's Manual of Method and Organisation, Adapted to the Primary Schools of Great Britain, Ireland, and the Colonies*, 3rd ed., Longmans (1st ed. published in 1863)
Robinson, W.P. and Rackstraw, S.J. (1972) *A Question of Answers*, 2 vols., Routledge and Kegan Paul, London
Rogers, S. (1976) 'The Language of Children and Adolescents and the Language of Schooling', in Rogers, S. (ed.), *They Don't Speak Our Language: Essays on the Language World of Children and Adolescents*, Edward Arnold, London
Rose, N. (1979) 'The Psychological Complex: Mental Measurement and Social Administration', *Ideology and Consciousness*, 5, 5–68
Rosen, H. (1974) *Language and Social Class: A Critical Look at the*

Theories of Basil Bernstein, 3rd ed., Falling Wall Press, Bristol (1st ed. published in 1972)

Runciman, J. (1887) *Schools and Scholars*, Chatto and Windus, London

Salmon, D. (1898) *The Art of Teaching*, Longmans, London

Sarlar, C. (1978) 'Class Test', *The Sunday Times*, 6 August 1978, p. 13

Schatzmann, L. and Strauss, A. (1955) 'Social Class and Modes of Communication', *American Journal of Sociology*, **60**, No. 4, 329–38

Schuster, E. [1913] *Eugenics*, Collins, London, n.d.

Scott-Giles, C.W. and Slater, B.V. (1966) *The History of Emanuel School 1594–1964*, The Old Emanuel Association, London

Searle, G.R. (1976) *Eugenics and Politics in Britain 1900–1914*, Noordhoff International Publishing, Leyden

Selleck, R.J.W. (1968) *The New Education 1870–1914*, Pitman, London

Shuy, R.W. and Fasold, R.W. (eds., 1973) *Language Attitudes: Current Trends and Prospects*, Georgetown University Press, Washington, DC

—— and Williams, F. (1973) 'Stereotyped Attitudes of Selected English Dialect Communities' in Shuy and Fasold (eds., 1973), pp. 85–96

Simon, B. (1949a) 'Science and Pseudo-Science in Psychology', *Education Bulletin*, October 1949, p. 12

—— (1949b) 'The Theory and Practice of Intelligence Testing', *Communist Review*, pp. 687–95

—— (1953) *Intelligence Testing and the Comprehensive School*, in Simon, B. (1978, pp. 29–121)

—— (1960) *Studies in the History of Education 1780–1870*, Lawrence and Wishart, London (Re-titled *The Two Nations and the Educational Structure 1780–1870* in 1974). (Simon, B. *Studies in the History of Education* [1780–1940], Vol. 1)

—— (1965) *Education and the Labour Movement 1870–1920*, Lawrence and Wishart, London (Simon, B., *Studies in the History of Education* [1780–1940], Vol. 2)

—— (1967) 'Classification and Streaming: A Study of Grouping in English Schools', in Simon, B. (1978), pp. 200–36

—— (1970) 'Intelligence, Race, Class and Education', in Simon, B. (1978), pp. 237–63

—— (1974) *The Politics of Educational Reform 1920–1940*, Lawrence and Wishart, London (Simon, B., *Studies in the History of Education* [1780–1940], Vol. 3)

—— (1976) 'Contemporary Problems in Educational Theory', in

Simon, B. (1978), pp. 264–81

Simon, B. (1978) *Intelligence, Psychology and Education: A Marxist Critique*, 2nd ed., Lawrence and Wishart, London (1st ed. published in 1971)

Simon, (Sir) E.D., Lady [S.D.] Simon, Robson, W.A. and Jewkes, J. (1937) *Moscow in the Making*, Longmans, London

Simon, J. (1949) 'Mental Testing', *Modern Quarterly*, NS 5, Pt 1, 19–37

Simon of Wythenshawe, Lady [S.D. Simon] (1948) *Three Schools or One? Secondary Education in England, Scotland and the USA*, Frederick Muller, London

Sinclair, J.McH. and Coulthard, R.M. (1975) *Towards an Analysis of Discourse: The English Used by Teachers and Pupils, based on a report submitted to the Social Science Research Council and written by J. McH. Sinclair, I.J. Forsyth, R.M. Coulthard and M.C. Ashby*, Oxford University Press, London

Smith, L.P. (1924) *Four Words: Romantic, Originality, Creative, Genius*, Oxford University Press, London (*Society for Pure English Tract*, 17)

Spencer, H. (1884) *Education: Intellectual, Moral, And Physical*, Williams and Norgate, London (1st ed. published in 1861)

Spens Report (1938) – See Official Publications

Stewart, W.A. (1970) 'Toward a History of American Negro Dialect', in Williams (ed., 1970), pp. 351–79

Stow, D. (1836) *The Training System Adopted in the Model Schools of the Glasgow Educational Society; A Manual for Infant and Juvenile Schools, which Includes a System of Moral Training Suited to the Condition of Large Towns*, W.R. M'Phun, Glasgow

Stubbs, M. (1975) 'Teaching and Talking: A Sociolinguistic Approach to Classroom Interaction', in Chanan and Delamont (eds., 1975), pp. 233–46

—— (1976a) *Language, Schools and Classrooms*, Methuen, London

—— (1976b) 'Keeping in Touch: Some Functions of Teacher-Talk', in Stubbs and Delamont (eds., 1976), pp. 151–72

—— (1980) *Language and Literacy: The Sociolinguistics of Reading and Writing*, Routledge and Kegan Paul, London

—— and Delamont, S. (eds., 1976) *Explorations in Classroom Observation*, Wiley, Chichester, Sussex

Sturt, M. (1967) *The Education of the People: A History of Primary Education in England and Wales in the Nineteenth Century*, Routledge and Kegan Paul, London

Sully, James (1897) *The Teacher's Handbook of Psychology*, 4th ed., Longmans, London (1st ed. published in 1886)

Sutherland, G. (1977) 'The Magic of Measurement: Mental Testing and English Education 1900–40', *Transactions of the Royal Historical Society*, 5th Series, Vol. 27, pp. 135–53

Sweet, H. (1891) *A New English Grammar, Logical and Historical. Part I: Introduction, Phonology, and Accidence*, Clarendon Press, Oxford

Tawney, R.H. (ed.) [1922] *Secondary Education for All: A Policy for Labour. Edited for the Education Advisory Committee of the Labour Party by R.H. Tawney*, The Labour Party and George Allen and Unwin, London, n.d.

—— (1931) *Equality*, 2nd ed., George Allen and Unwin, London (1st ed. published in 1931)

Taylor [of Stanford Rivers], I. (1842) *Home Education . . .* , 4th ed., Jackson and Walford, London (1st ed. published in 1838)

Taylor, O.L. (1973) 'Teachers' Attitudes toward Black and Non-Standard English as Measured by the Language Attitude Scale', in Shuy and Fasold (eds., 1973), pp. 174–201

Templin, M.C. (1957) *Certain Language Skills in Children: Their Development and Interrelationships*, University of Minnesota Press, Minneapolis

Thomson, (Sir) G.H. (1929) *A Modern Philosophy of Education*, George Allen and Unwin, London

Tough, J. (1976) *Listening to Children Talking: A Guide to the Appraisal of Children's Use of Language*, Ward Lock Educational in association with Drake Educational Associates, London (*Schools Council Communication Skills in Early Childhood Project*)

—— (1977) *The Development of Meaning: A Study of Children's Use of Language*, George Allen and Unwin, London

Traugott, E.C. (1976) 'Pidgins, Creoles, and the Origins of Vernacular Black English', in Harrison, D.S. and Trabasso, T. (eds.), *Black English: A Seminar*, Lawrence Erlbaum Associates, Hillsdale, New Jersey, pp. 57–93

Trudgill, P. (1975) *Accent, Dialect and the School*, Edward Arnold, London

—— and Giles, H. (1976) *Sociolinguistics and Linguistic Value Judgements: Correctness, Adequacy and Aesthetics*, Linguistic Agency University of Trier, April 1976 (Series B, Paper 10)

Turner, G.J. (1973) 'Social Class and Children's Language of Control at Age Five and Age Seven', in Bernstein (ed., 1973), pp. 135–201

Tyler, W. (1977) *The Sociology of Educational Inequality*, Methuen, London

Unwin, W.J. (1862) *The Primary School, First Part: School Management*, Longman Green, Longman and Roberts, London

Vernon, P.E. (ed., 1957) *Secondary School Selection: A British Psychological Society Inquiry*, Methuen, London

—— (1978) *Intelligence: Heredity and Environment*, W.H. Freeman, San Francisco

Vygotsky, L.S. (1962) *Thought and Language*, ed. and translated by E. Hanfmann and G. Vakar, MIT Press, Cambridge, Mass. (Original version first published in Russian in 1934)

Wade, D. (1963) 'S[ixth] F[orm] O[pinion] Poll. "If I were an M.P." Results analysed by the Editor, Dyan Wade', *Sixth Form Opinion*, 5, 27–30

Wales, K. (1978) 'Further Notes on Personal Reference in Colloquial English', *UEA Papers in Linguistics*, 7, 1–10

Ward, H. and Roscoe, F. (1928) *The Approach to Teaching*, G. Bell, London

Wells, G. (1977) 'Language Use and Educational Success: A Response to Joan Tough's *The Development of Meaning*', *Nottingham Linguistic Circular*, 6, No. 2, 29–50

Welton, J. (1911) *The Psychology of Education*, Macmillan, London

—— (1915) *What Do We Mean by Education?*, Macmillan, London

Whitten, Jr, N.E. and Szwed, J.F. (eds., 1970) *Afro-American Anthropology: Contemporary Perspectives*, Free Press, New York

Whorf, B.L. (1940a) 'Science and Linguistics', in Carroll (ed., 1956), pp. 207–19

—— (1940b) 'Linguistics as an Exact Science', in Carroll (ed., 1956), pp. 220–32

—— (1942) 'Language, Mind and Reality', in Carroll (ed., 1956), pp. 246–70

Wilderspin, S. (1840) *A System for the Education of the Young, Applied to All the Faculties; Founded on Immense Experience of Many Thousands of Children, in Most Parts of the Three Kingdoms. With an Appendix and Plates*, James S. Hudson, at the Depot for American Literature, London

Wilkinson, A.M. (1971) *The Foundations of Language: Talking and Reading in Young Children*, OUP, London

Williams, F. (1970) 'Some Preliminaries and Prospects', in Williams (ed., 1970), pp. 1–10

—— (ed., 1970) *Language and Poverty: Perspectives on a Theme*,

Markham Publishing, Chicago

Williams, F. (1973) 'Some Research Notes on Dialect Attitudes and Stereotypes', in Shuy and Fasold (eds., 1973), pp. 113–28

Wilson, A. (1908) *Education, Personality and Crime: A Practical Treatise Built up on Scientific Details, Dealing with Difficult Social Problems*, Greening, London

Wimms, J.H. (1915) *An Introduction to Psychology for the Use of Teachers*, 3rd ed., Charles and Son, London (1st ed. published in 1908)

Wooler, W.M. [1859] *Physiology of Education: Comprising a Compendious Cyclopaedia of Mental, Moral and Social Facts*, Simpkin, Marshall and Co., London, n.d.

III. Published Tape-recordings

Lee, V. and Bernstein, B. (1977) *Code and Context*, Open University Educational Enterprises, Stony Stratford, Milton Keynes, Buckinghamshire 1977 (Tape E262/04)

INDEX

Adams, Sir John 30, 35, 46n21, 134, 135, *see also* Herbartians
Adlam, D.S. 89n21

Bagley, W.C. 35
Bailey, Beryl L. 97
Bain, A. 134, 135
Ballard, P.B. 34
Banks, Olive 87n3, 109
Baratz, Joan 42, 96, 98–9, 100, 101
Baratz, Stephen 42, 96, 98
Barlow, Montague 45n19
Barnes, Douglas 108, 152
Barnett, P.A. 134
Bartley, Sir G.C.T. 134, 135
Belcourt, Susanne 108
Benson, A.C. 134, 135
Bereiter, Carl 49, 53–6, 64n5, 97
Bernstein, Basil: cited in classical verbal deficit theory 49, 56; early papers (1958–61) 68–74; later papers (1962–73) 74–81; skirmishes with Labov 90; some experiments conducted by 71, 75–6, 83–4; *see also* Bernstein's theory: affinities with Norwood ideology 123; affinities with psychometric intelligence theory 121–3; as account for differential educational attainment 73, 81–2, 86; as verbal deficit theory 48–9, 66, 83–6, 114; climate favouring reception 120–3, 125–6; codes (elaborated and restricted) 74–81, defined in terms of implicitness and explicitness 76–7, defined in terms of syntactic predictability 74–6, linguistic dimension 74–8, psychological dimension 78–9, sociological dimension 74, 79–80; concept of social class 72; interpretations: Leonard Jackson's 82–3, others 81–2; obscurities 66–7, 86; public and formal language 68–71; reception among teachers 110–11, 113n11–12, 137; untestable 71, 73, 86; *see also* Basil Bernstein

bi-dialectalism 101–2, 103, 123, 129n15
Birchenough, Charles 44n2, 44n13, 45n18, 45n19
Black English Vernacular (BEV) 54–5, 96–7, 112n4
Black Papers 117, 128n4
Blakiston, J.R. 39, 134
Boultwood, M.E.A. 28
'bourgeois values of the school' 105–7
Boydell, Deanne 108
Boyle, Sir Edward (Lord Boyle of Handsworth) 46n20
Bray, S.E. 135
Bullock Report (1975) 109
Burling, R. 64n3
Burt, Sir Cyril 30, 32, 33, 34, 35; and Norwood ideology 36–7, 129n14

Calderwood, H. 134
Carroll, J.B. 65n13
Cassidy, F.G. 97
Cazden, Courtney B. 96
Chanan, Gabriel 42, 107, 112n9, 112n10
child-centred education 29–30
Chomsky, Noam 77, 111n3
Clarke, A.D.B. 111n1, 129n13
Clarke, Ann 129n13
Clarke, Sir Fred 38–9, 41
classroom interaction 108, 113n10, 151–4
Collar, G. 134
Collins, G. 44n15, 134
Collins, R.N. 24, 134
Combe, G. 133
compulsory school attendance 45n18
Cook-Gumperz, Jenny 89n21
Coulthard, Malcolm 71, 75, 90, 108, 110
Coupland, W.C. 134, 136
Cowham, J.H. 134
Cox, T.A. 134
Creber, J.W.P. 109
Crook, C.W. 134

176